Arabian Nightmare

Arabian Nightmare

RICHARD ARNOT

with Helen Chryssides

A Sue Hines Book
ALLEN & UNWIN

First published in 1999
A Sue Hines Book
Allen & Unwin Pty Ltd
9 Atchison Street
St Leonards, NSW 1590, Australia
19 Compton Terrace
London N1 2UN
Phone: (61 2) 8425 0100
Fax: (61 2) 9906 2218
E-mail: frontdesk@allen-unwin.com.au
Web: http://www.allen-unwin.com.au

ISBN 1 86448 647 3

British Library Cataloguing-in-Publication Data

A CIP record for this book is available from the British Library

Typeset by J & M Typesetting
Cover photograph by David Seidner
Cover and text design by Ruth Grüner
Printed and bound in Great Britain by Biddles Ltd.,
Guildford & King's Lynn

1 3 5 7 9 10 8 6 4 2

◻◻◻

This book is dedicated to my love, Margaret, who saved my sanity in 1981, and has given unstinting love and support ever since, and our three children, who have made it all worthwhile. It is also dedicated to my children William and Lucy in the expectation that they will understand, and to my first wife Penelope, whose nightmare was worse than mine.

Contents

◰◱◰

Acknowledgements

I started writing this book in 1980, but the events of 1979 were too fresh and painful to make sense, and it was only in 1996 that I was finally able to complete the manuscript after many false starts. This book would not have been possible had it not been for the enthusiasm and hard work of Helen Chryssides who, with the help of my diaries and many hours of interviews and my original manuscript, turned it all into a gripping story.

Before her, my brother-in-law Paul Johnson had given me ideas for a start. I should like to thank the unknown book editor who took the time to advise me to advertise for a writer, and thus led me to Philippa Sandall who, in turn, introduced me to Margaret Connolly who became my agent, and helped to make this all happen.

Margaret introduced me to Sue Hines, who had the confidence to convince Allen & Unwin that this was a story they could not afford to miss.

Thanks are also due to Jamie Anderson, who tirelessly edited the manuscript and added his encyclopaedic knowledge of the Middle-East to provide the detail it needed to complete the stage on which this true story is set. I am also grateful to Doug Sturkey who kindly reviewed the manuscript despite completing a busy schedule at Yarralumla House.

My endless thanks are due to my wife Margaret, and our three children, who supported me and put up with Dad's dark and silent moods while I was writing this. Finally I have to thank my prison visitors – Angela, Judy, Pip and Sharon – who braved the chaos and throng of black-cowled women in Jeddah to help break the monotony of prison life, and John and Sue Onslow, who gave us the shelter when we were most in need.

One night, in Arabia

'Wake up! Richard, wake up!'

My wife Penny is shaking me.

'Hurry, quickly, wake up! I think something terrible has happened.'

Heat. Light. Noise. Penny has me by the shoulders. I open my eyes and flinch in the brightness. It is early morning in Jeddah, Saudi Arabia.

Penny's expression is shocked. Her face is ashen. Her voice is trembling. She is still wearing the white blouse and blue denim jeans she had on at the party we held the night before. She obviously has not been to bed. Behind her stand Tim Hayter, a diver from New Zealand, and a Frenchman – what is his name – Jacques. They, too, appear stunned.

'I think something terrible has happened,' Penny says again, frantically.

'What do you mean?'

'I think Helen has fallen off the balcony.'

After only three and a half hours' sleep, and despite the remaining effects of several whiskies, I was instantly alert. Doctors are used to being woken in the middle of the night and pushed urgently into action.

For all the efforts of the air conditioner, my body felt clammy. I was bathed in sweat. I leapt out of bed, wrapped a towel around my waist and ran to the balcony. Its railing was less than eighty centimetres high, not reaching far above my knee.

In the courtyard, more than twenty metres beneath me, sprawled a motionless female form. It was 5.30 a.m. There was enough light in the early morning to make out the woman's light-coloured dress. I gasped in horror. And the nightmare began.

I dashed back inside the room and grabbed a shirt, trousers and sandals. I dressed quickly, and ran down the six flights of stairs. There was a lift, but it was utterly unreliable and out of action more often than not. I did not give it a second glance but instead pounded down the stairs. This was no time to get stuck in an elevator.

I was making rational decisions but my anxiety was increasing with each step.

Helen? Could the body really be Helen's?

Helen, who was a friend of our family. Helen, who had cups of tea and chats with Penny and babysat for us. Helen, adored by our young children, William and Lucy. Helen, with whom I had laughed and joked for several hours at the party last night. Just three and a half hours ago. Helen was only a girl. So young, so full of life.

But I am a doctor. Doctors respond to emergency with action. People expect it. People demand it. When blood flows, doctors clamp and suture. They cope. Sometimes, despite all their clamping and suturing, the patient dies. Doctors have to cope with that, too.

Out of breath, I reached the bottom of the stairs. From the main door of the block of flats I ran down the five steps to the pavement. I turned right and then right again, into the enclosed space between the security fence on the street and the building.

I saw him first. A large muscular body. There, in the alley between the security fence and the front of the building, an area no more than two metres wide, the body of a man was impaled on railings.

The sight of the body struck me like a blow.

His head and shoulders were drooped over the white iron pickets and two or three spikes protruded from his lower back. The man's arms were hanging down by his side. His head was covered by clothing. His white shirt was unbuttoned and virtually off him, just hanging on by the sleeves. His legs were hanging over the pavement side of the fence, his underpants draped around his ankles. His genitals, enlarged and distended, were in full view.

The body was still dripping a little blood. A pool of the vivid red congealed liquid lay on the ground below his head. A trail of large black ants scurried to and fro. He was dead. For sure. It took me only a fraction of a second to take it all in as I recoiled in horror.

Turning around then, I saw her. It was Helen. My heart sank. A couple of metres away by the front wall of the building, she was lying on her side. Her dress had ridden up, exposing her bare buttocks. Her knickers were around one leg. Her left arm was bent and covering her face, as if to keep the sun out of her eyes. Her eyes were closed and she had a little dent on her forehead.

She looked as if she might just be asleep. She looked as if she might not be dead. She seemed to be merely napping.

A sudden flash of hope shot through me and I dropped to my knees. I reached out for her wrist, and went to feel her pulse. But her arm was stiff and her skin cold to the touch. She was dead and I could do nothing for her.

Thinking like a pathologist, I moved her head slightly and checked her pupils. I concluded that she had been dead for some time. An hour and a half? Two hours? But that was a secondary reaction. I was first a doctor, confirming death, vaguely aware that I should look for some obvious cause.

There was no blood to be seen. The only mark I noticed was a slight dent on her forehead. I thought she had probably struck her head during the fall.

A sudden memory flashed into my mind of three young women who had died, with barely a mark on them, in a high speed car crash I had attended in Britain. Could Helen, like them, have struck at such velocity that she suffered fatal internal injury? I gave up the memory. My responsibility here was not to conduct a post mortem but to confirm death.

I had done that for Helen. Now I turned my attention to the man.

His body appeared to be folded over the fence. The metal railing running near the top of the pickets from one post to the next, was bent and partly pulled away from the posts. It sagged with the weight of the body. One of the lamps, the one on top of the post nearest the building, was hanging loose, torn away from its concrete base, but the glass was not broken.

His upper body pointed away from the building, towards the street. The spikes had penetrated the front of the lower part of his abdomen. I did not recognise his swollen face, which was engorged with blood. After death, blood flows according to gravity and pools in the lowest parts of a body. His white shirt was unbuttoned. It hung down behind his head like a curtain.

I shuddered in horror. But again my immediate and overwhelming concern was as a doctor. I felt his pulse. There was no response. He was wearing a wristwatch. This body, too, was stiff and cool to the touch. He was plainly dead.

He was not wearing trousers, merely underpants. They were down around his ankles. The most striking feature of the body from this angle was the penis, enlarged and distended. He wore neither shoes nor socks.

In the split second it had taken me to survey the scene, and to see the bodies and the way they were lying, half-dressed, I immediately assumed they had been having sex and had gone over the balcony. It just seemed so obvious. There could be no other explanation.

The whole process, from my time of awakening, to the confirmation of the two deaths, had taken only a few minutes. My mind was now catching up with my actions and as I began to make my way back up to the flat, sickened and nauseated by what I had seen, the implications of these terrible events began to crystallise in my mind.

We had held a party in my flat. We had consumed a considerable amount of alcohol. Under Saudi law, the consumption of alcohol was strictly forbidden, even in the privacy of one's own home. We knew we were taking a risk.

Most Europeans in Saudi Arabia took the same risk. Providing discretion was observed, it was relatively safe. But our party was about to be thrust into a very harsh spotlight. There had been two deaths. The police would be called. There would be questions about the party and, naturally, whether or not there had been alcohol. I was immediately and vividly aware that we had to take steps to protect ourselves. In the meantime, the others obviously had had the same thought.

I arrived back upstairs to find Penny standing pale and trembling, smoking agitatedly, as Tim and Jacques emptied bottles of Johnnie Walker down the kitchen sink.

They turned to me in anticipation.

'You're right. It is Helen and she's dead.'

'Oh my God,' cried Penny, bursting into tears.

'There's also another body. A man. He fell on to the railings.'

'What? How can that be?'

'Who is it?'

'I have no idea. What happened last night? What happened after I went to bed?' I blurted out. 'How did Helen fall over the balcony?'

'I don't know, Richard. I don't know,' sobbed Penny. 'The last I saw of her, she was on the balcony with Johannes. The others left without them. They thought that Helen and Johannes must have gone off somewhere together –'

Tim chipped in, 'Johannes, of course, that's who the other body is.'

'Then go and check,' I said.

Tim ran down the stairs while Penny and Jacques rapidly filled me in on the closing stages of the party.

'We just talked on and danced. Then people started to leave.'

'What about Helen and Johannes?'

'I told you, Richard. The last we saw of them, they were going out on to the balcony.'

'When the others wanted to go home, they looked for Helen and Johannes,' added Jacques. 'They could not find them. So they left without them.'

'They looked for them? But you said Helen and Johannes were on the balcony.'

'Yes, we saw them go out on the balcony but when the others looked, they weren't there any more. So we thought they must have come in by the other door and gone to Helen's flat.'

'You saw how the two of them were getting on, Richard.'

'Yes, yes, I know. Then what?'

'Well, no one was concerned or worried. If they wanted to go off together, that wasn't anyone else's business. The Germans left. I started to clear up and then we all went to sleep. I made some coffee when I woke up this morning. Tim and I went on to the balcony to watch the sun rise and . . .'

Tim returned, visibly shaken, to confirm the worst. 'Yes, that's Johannes.'

Of course. Helen and Johannes had been getting on very well at the party, very well indeed. I had noticed them dancing together closely as I left for an early night before morning surgery. They must later have gone on to the balcony to get amorous. Both having had a bit to drink, they must then have fallen over the low railing.

The balcony railing that, time after time, we had asked be raised to a safe height. In the end it was not our children but two adults who had come to grief.

'It's awful, unbelievable,' Tim continued.

'Hideous,' I agreed.

'And what's happened to his trousers?'

'Goodness knows. Maybe they came off as he fell and –'

But there was no time for speculation. We had a pressing problem.

'Quick, we have to get rid of the alcohol and call the police.'

I am sure it sounds callous that upon discovering two bodies, one a friend of the family, our attention should first have turned to ridding the house of alcohol.

The deaths were shocking, and stunning – but to have done nothing except grieve did not occur to any of us. Our right to live and work in Saudi Arabia had been thrown into question. As well, we were still working in the emotional vacuum that follows any sudden shock.

Now getting rid of the liquor left over from the party seemed paramount. There had been two deaths and we may be held responsible. Stored in the second toilet, we had a sixty-litre bin full of the most marvellous wine. It had partly fermented and was almost ready to be bottled. In Saudi, home-made wine was a cheap alternative to black market scotch.

On our first visit to the local supermarket, Penny and I had been astonished to find an entire section devoted to winemaking. Next to the bottles of pasteurised grape juice, were plastic tubing and large containers with taps in their side. There was a section selling yeast. There were large bags of sugar. All one would ever need to survive in an alcohol-free country.

The Frenchman, the New Zealander and I struggled to the bathroom with the bin of fermenting wine. We poured its contents down the drain, almost reeling from the strong fumes. While we were busy with this process, there was a knock at the door.

'What's that?'

'Someone at the door. What can they want?'

'Open the door, Richard,' said Tim, the New Zealand diver.

'Maybe we should ignore it. Whoever it is will go away. Surely?'

The knocking began again.

'Open the door.'

We whispered on for a few seconds. We were far from ready for visitors.

Finally, tentatively, I opened the door a few centimetres.

Dr Abdul Rakhman, a Sudanese doctor who lived in the ground floor flat, stood on the landing. He was accompanied by the Saudi janitor/caretaker whom I knew from past encounters could not speak English.

'Do you know there are two bodies beneath your balcony?' asked Dr Rakhman grimly. The caretaker looked on, clearly panic-stricken.

'Yes, yes, I know,' I snapped. 'The matter is in hand. We are taking care of it.'

I dismissed them rather abruptly, and closed the door.

'Who was it?'

'Dr Abdul Rakhman, with the building caretaker. They've found the bodies.'

'How did they know to come here?'

'Perhaps they saw you examining the bodies.'

'Perhaps.'

I decided on a new course of action. I asked Jacques and Tim to continue cleaning up, while I went to the nearest phone – at Bakhsh Hospital where I worked – to call the police. Again, I rushed down the stairs, then ran along the road to the casualty department of the hospital.

'Quick, I need to make an urgent telephone call,' I told the startled nurse.

Dialling the number with trembling fingers, I first rang Dr Bakhsh, the owner of the hospital.

'It's Richard Arnot here. I'm calling you because there's been a terrible accident. Two people are dead. Helen Smith, a nurse at your hospital, is one of them. She fell off the balcony of my flat after a party last night.'

I stated the facts in precise terms. I spoke in what I thought was a clear and direct manner. But there was no response.

I repeated the news. Dr Bakhsh, a Pakistani by birth, spoke English, but he was not fluent and at times of high emotion or in awkward situations, he either could not or would not understand.

Wiping the sweat from my forehead in frustration, I turned to see Dr Sukhtian, an Armenian orthopaedic surgeon, who occupied the flat next to ours.

'Can I help?' he asked me brusquely.

'Please,' I gasped, 'please can you explain to Dr Bakhsh what has happened; that two people are dead. One of them is Helen Smith –'

Quickly I told Dr Sukhtian the details. He took the receiver from my hand and spoke rapidly to Dr Bakhsh in Arabic.

'And please, also call the police.'

'Yes, Dr Bakhsh says they must be informed.'

'Of course, but I cannot do it. I have very little Arabic, as you know, and the police speak no English.'

I glanced up at the clock on the wall as he made the call. It was 5.50 a.m.

'The police are on their way,' he assured me as he put down the receiver.

'Thank you. Thank you very much,' I told Dr Sukhtian. 'I will go back to the flat and wait for them.'

As I walked towards my apartment block, I noticed a small, green-coloured object lying on the roadway. Early morning traffic was building, and it was obvious that whatever the green thing was it would soon be run over and damaged. So I picked it up.

It was Johannes' passport.

Making a mental note of the spot where I had found the passport, I placed it on the pavement by his feet.

'The police will be here shortly,' I told Penny. All the alcohol had by now been poured or flushed away and the empty whisky bottles rinsed and stored in a bag in a cupboard in the children's bedroom. Tim and Jacques were leaving. Tim was on his way back to the barge on which he was employed as a salvage diver. Jacques returned to the boat where he lived, on a creek off Jeddah Harbour.

'We should wake the children and tell them what has happened,' I told Penny once the two men had gone. That was a task I did not relish. Of the several women who looked after them, Helen had been their favourite babysitter. It would be difficult to break the news.

Painfully contemplating that, I was at the same time hit by the realisation that the immediate future of Penny and myself, and therefore of our children, was unclear, to say the least.

At just eight and six years of age, William and Lucy were already capable and self-reliant children. But I knew they would have to gather all the strength in their small bodies to cope with the frightening news.

Lucy was already conscious, having been roused by the clinking of empty bottles being stashed in the top shelf of the cupboard of her bedroom. William, harder to disturb, slept blissfully on.

'William darling, time to get up,' I said to my sleeping son as Penny gently stroked him on the shoulder. William sat up, struggling to wake. Lucy, alert and sitting up had grasped that something serious was happening.

We did not beat around the bush. I came straight to the point. 'Children, something terrible has happened. Helen has fallen off the balcony and is dead. Mummy and I have to talk to the police. They are on their way. Mummy and I may have to go with them to answer some questions.'

The children responded with blank expressions, seemingly unable to comprehend the enormity of what we were telling them. Lucy however understood that her friend Helen had died, and a tear trickled down her cheek.

'Where are the police?' I asked myself frantically. 'Where are they?'

Leaving Penny in the bedroom with the children, I stepped out onto the balcony once more. There were people below.

'I'm going back downstairs,' I told Penny, 'it looks as if Dr Bakhsh may have arrived.'

It was just after 6.00 a.m.

I was anxious to speak to Dr Bakhsh before the police arrived. What were we to say to them about the alcohol? He would obviously have a much clearer insight about their attitude in these circumstances.

After I explained our predicament to him, Dr Bakhsh looked me straight in the eye. 'You must be completely frank with the police,' he told me. 'There is nothing to fear with regard to the drinking.'

Another thought suddenly struck me. Should I contact anyone else? Yes, yes, the embassy. I should let them know what was happening too. I knew the implications of the affair were serious, and

I did not like the prospect of facing the Saudi authorities without the backing of the British Embassy.

I hurried back to my office at the hospital and phoned the only official I knew at the embassy, Colonel Murray de Klee, the military attaché. A man of few words at the best of times, de Klee grunted that he would contact the duty officer and get a British Embassy official to immediately attend the scene.

'Richard.'

I looked up from my desk to see Agnes Johnstone, the matron of the Bakhsh Hospital and a good friend.

'Richard, I heard there had been an accident and –' Agnes was in a state of anxiety.

'Helen's dead. She fell off the balcony.'

'No, no, no –'

As I put my arms out to comfort Agnes, I began to weep myself.

It was a little like coming home and telling your mother there had been an accident at school. You keep it all inside until you have someone you feel close to. For me, that someone was Agnes. And, having blurted it out to her, I broke down too and was able to shed my first tears.

'I have to get back to the flat,' I spluttered. 'Penny is waiting – the police are on their way.'

'Yes, yes, Richard, go.'

Sweat was pouring off me by the time I got back to the flat. The children were up and dressed. I sank into a chair. Penny seemed to have successfully cleared the debris from the party. If I thought about it at all, I assumed that Penny must have begun to clean up as soon as the guests had left the night before. The flat was remarkably tidy. Too tidy, as it turned out.

Now there was only the waiting, and the time to think. It was an intolerable period. Everything that could be done had been done.

'Daddy, are we going to school?' asked Lucy.

'There is no school today, darling.'

'Can we go outside and play?' William wanted to know.

'Please, yes, please can we go outside and play?'

'Stop it! Be quiet!' snapped Penny. 'I can't stand this. Where are they? Where are the police? What's taking so long?'

'Daddy, I'm scared,' whimpered Lucy.

'Hush, hush, it's all right. It's all right.'

'Are the police going to take you away?' asked William.

'No!' shrieked Lucy, 'No!'

'No one is going to take us away. Just stay calm, children, stay calm. It's going to be all right.'

The police finally arrived at half past six. There were six officers in two Toyota Land Cruisers. They were dressed in bottle green uniforms, black berets on their heads, pistols strapped to their sides. I went downstairs to the street to meet them.

Time was made to perform the usual Arab courtesies; an exchange of the blessings of Allah. Then, with Dr Bakhsh volunteering himself as interpreter, the questioning began.

In a voice as strong and clear as I could make it, I recounted, for the first of many times, what had happened.

'We held a party at our flat on the sixth floor last night. There were several people, and –' I hesitated. Dr Bakhsh frowned at me. I gulped. Taking a deep breath, I continued. 'There were several people at the party, about ten or so, and we – we drank alcohol.'

While I told the story of the party to the police, in the street around us, a small crowd had gathered. There was much pointing at Johannes' body, in its naked, aroused state. There were guffaws, ribald laughter. After an initial grimace, the police themselves smiled.

Interrupting the police examination, Dr Bakhsh snapped a few words at a young man who strode away purposefully.

'What did you say?'

'I told him to get some sheets from the hospital to cover up the bodies.'

I averted my gaze from Johannes and down to the ground.

'This is Johannes Otten's passport. I found it on the road. Just over there,' I pointed. 'It must have fallen out of his trouser pocket.'

'Where are his trousers?'

'I don't know.'

One of the policemen, a rather dandified individual, who seemed excessively self-aware, and whom we later nicknamed 'Pretty Boy', took charge of the questioning.

I continued with my account, 'At some stage towards the end of the party, Helen Smith and Johannes Otten went out on to the balcony. They were not seen again. The others thought they had left the party and so were not anxious about them. Then, this morning, we found the bodies.'

'Where is your family now?' asked the policeman.

'In the flat upstairs.'

'Bring them down and take them to the hospital,' he ordered.

I did as I was told.

Silently I led Penny, William and Lucy down the stairs and on to the street. Lucy was clutching an ancient bear called Pink Andrew. Christmas, the stray cat, was apparently forgotten. As we left the apartment block and passed the bodies, which were now mercifully hidden by sheets from the hospital, both children glanced curiously at the scene.

Apart from the sheeted bodies, the only visible sign of anything amiss was the pool of blood on the glazed tiles beneath Johannes' body. When, years later, I asked Lucy about her recollection of that morning, it was the sight of the little pool of congealed blood that had stuck in her memory.

At the time, part of me wondered what effect this day would have on my children – viewing such a grotesque scene, walking through the group of stern policemen and inquisitive, mocking onlookers? Would they remember it in years to come? Would the images return to haunt and frighten them?

Penny went with them to the hospital to wait.

A few minutes later the officials from the embassy arrived. Two men whom I had never previously met, Gordon Kirby and Mike Baumer, introduced themselves. Their very British presence – jackets, white shirts and ties – was instantly reassuring.

'Mr Arnot, the duty officer said –'

Pretty Boy instantly stood between us, snapping in his rough English. 'No talk. No talk.'

Gordon Kirby, who turned out to be the vice-consul, approached the bodies. Then, positioning himself in front of me, he mumbled out of the corner of his mouth, 'What happened?'

'They fell – balcony. We – party last night – alcohol – sixth floor –'

The policeman realised we were breaking his code of silence. Bristling with indignation, he dismissed the embassy officials with a summary wave of his hand.

'Must go!' Pretty Boy ordered.

As he left, Kirby managed to ask, 'Where's your wife?'

'At the hospital.' As a sudden afterthought, I added, 'Tell her to drink lots of water.'

'What?'

'Water, tell her to drink lots of water,' I hissed. 'To get rid of the alcohol.' For surely we would be tested for that.

'Must go!' repeated the policeman, vehemently.

My heart pounded in panic as the two men walked away. I felt abandoned by my compatriots, isolated. My concern increased as I caught sight of Dr Bakhsh's austere expression. He looked angry, enraged, no doubt contemplating the shame and humiliation I had brought upon his beloved hospital. I would get little support, much less sympathy, from him.

And why should I even expect it? We had, after all, never enjoyed a close working relationship. Instead of mutual support, there had been constant friction between us. I had never considered him an ally then. Why should I consider him to be one now?

No, I was alone in Saudi Arabia, without an advocate.

As the British Embassy officials left, two more police vehicles arrived, doubling the Saudi police contingent. Among the new arrivals was a police photographer who, with a huge single lens reflex camera, snapped picture after picture of the two bodies.

His actions prompted my memory. I'm a typical party shutterbug and I had snapped a few candid pictures on the previous evening. Should I tell the police?

For a very long time, I stood around on the pavement, feeling futile, unable to communicate, lost in my thoughts, and having precious little idea of what was happening.

So finally, I was relieved to see someone I knew, however slightly, approaching. He was a young German by the name of Martin Fleischer. A university student, he was in Saudi Arabia for a few weeks of study and had been at our party. Fortunately for me, he spoke excellent English.

An hour or so earlier, on returning to the barge where he lived, Tim Hayter had woken Martin and told him of the deaths. Tim had then asked Martin to go and inform Harry Goodside, the boss of their diving team, and also a guest at our party.

Now Martin Fleischer was asking me, 'Where's Harry? I must tell him.'

'Harry? I have no idea,' I replied.

'But I thought he was with you.'

Martin informed me he had left the party at 2.30 a.m. or thereabouts, not long after I had gone to bed.

Harry Goodside left at approximately 3.15 a.m., shortly before the last guests, who had departed some fifteen minutes later.

'Tim told me Harry was in the flat.'

'Yes, but his own flat, not here. He lives in another part of town.'

'Oh. Do you know where?'

But before I could answer, Pretty Boy came up and demanded to know who this new arrival was.

'Martin Fleischer. He was at the party last night.'

Suddenly there was great interest; who else had been at the party? The police wanted names.

Martin and I sat down on the kerb and, with a pen in one hand, and the police notebook balanced on my knee, I wrote down the names as Martin called them out, one by one.

'Martin Fleischer, Harry Goodside, Manfred Schlafer –'

Martin's help was absolutely essential in this task. A number of people whom I did not know had been at the party.

I had formed an acquaintance with Tim Hayter because of my interest in scuba diving. I was only too happy for him to bring along his diving workmates for this party to celebrate the start of his leave.

'Klaus Ritter, Dieter Chapuis. Those are all the people from the Harms Salvage Company, Richard.' Harms was a German company working on extension and deepening of Jeddah Harbour.

While Martin was reeling off the names, I thought of another.

Pen poised, I remembered Alan, who had supplied the Johnnie Walker whisky. If we were to find ourselves in trouble for having drunk the stuff, he would be in much deeper water for having supplied it. But when it came to harmless old Johnnie Walker, I had all the time in the world for pushers and believed they should be protected. Alan was a good friend, just doing us a favour. And he had left the party well before midnight.

So, I left him off the list altogether. Instead, I wrote down, 'Tim Hayter, Jacques – (I couldn't think of his surname), Penny Arnot and Richard Arnot.'

Another name I omitted was that of a German who had arrived early and left almost as early. I did not know his name and I didn't believe merely dropping in at a party warranted the repercussions that seemed likely to befall the rest of us.

'That's it,' I concluded, 'there's the list.'

'These are the people that were at the party,' I told Pretty Boy, as I handed him the list.

'We must talk to them,' Pretty Boy replied. He looked at Martin. 'You know where they are?' Martin nodded. 'Get them,' he ordered, ushering Martin towards a police car.

Then he switched his gaze from the sheet covering Johannes

Otten's body to me. He was still obsessed by one puzzling aspect of the macabre scene; the absence of Johannes' trousers. 'Where are the trousers?'

'I told you. I do not know.'

'We must find the trousers.'

He decided it was time to search the flat.

I mounted the stairs tensely, followed by a contingent of police. They greeted our tidy flat with consternation. They seemed to find something sinister in its neatness.

Once more, I had to speak through Dr Bakhsh.

'My wife Penny cleared up after the last guests left the party.'

'What time was that?'

'Umm, about 3.30 I believe.'

'Where is the balcony?' asked Pretty Boy.

I took them out on to it, pointing out the two doors leading to it, and they examined the railing. I, too, looked for any sign of structural damage where Helen might have hit her head. I was still coming to terms with the memory that the only injury I had seen on her was that indentation on her forehead.

The Mini and the three young women had flashed into my mind when I noticed the small mark on Helen's forehead. At the accident I had attended years before in England, a Mini Minor had been involved in a head-on with a Jaguar. The occupants of the Mini – three young women – were sitting upright in the car seats with not a mark on them. Yet they were all of them dead due to a phenomenon called deceleration injury. When a body travelling at speed comes to an abrupt halt, the result may be fatal damage to internal organs. My mind had clicked into associating with that scene when I first saw Helen lying on the ground.

Pretty Boy left the balcony and re-entered the flat.

'I took some photographs at the party last night,' I told him.

'Where is the camera?'

He took it from me, and handed it to another officer for safe-keeping. I never saw the camera or the film again.

The policemen continued to inspect the flat.

I pointed out whatever seemed useful to their inquiries. 'Look, here are Helen's sandals and Johannes' shoes.' They had left them inside the small reception area by the front door of our flat when they arrived at the party.

I also found Johannes' glasses, Helen's handbag and her *abaya*, the black outer garment worn by Arab women when they leave the house. Many expatriate women in Jeddah observed this custom. Helen, by virtue of a few Arab boyfriends, had more reason to do so than most.

Following the police scrutiny of the flat, we returned to the street. Again, we seemed to spend an interminable amount of time waiting around on the pavement. The Saudis did not seem nearly as obsessed by time as we Westerners. They did not seem in the least perturbed about having to sit around and wait. In God's good time, what we are waiting for will come about. We waited until nearly half past ten, at least four hours from the time the police had arrived on the scene.

Finally, as my increasing anxiety was turning into frustration, Penny was brought back from the hospital and we were ordered into the same police car. This appeared to be an acknowledgement that we were related.

On the short journey to the police station, Penny told me about her interview with Gordon Kirby of the embassy.

'Where's your passport?' Kirby had asked.

'Here,' she said, producing it from her handbag and handing it over to him.

'If the Saudi police should ask for it, tell them it has been at the British Embassy for some days, awaiting a stamp,' he told her. 'Where is your husband's passport?' he continued.

'I don't know,' Penny had answered. Then a member of the hospital staff indicated a desk where all passports were kept. 'But they are not to be touched,' he informed the vice-consul.

At this point, Kirby apparently assumed an officious British demeanour and proceeded to impound my passport whereupon the hospital staff member left the room.

Minutes later, as Kirby was leaving, Dr Bakhsh stormed out of the hospital after him. 'You must return the passport,' he demanded.

That incident would certainly not have improved my personal or professional relations with the head of the hospital, I thought quietly to myself as we drove on, Penny grasping my hand anxiously.

'Who's looking after the children?' I asked.

'I've asked Gordon Kirby to take them to Judy Hindle's for the day,' she replied. Judy was a family friend, another British expat.

'What's going to happen now?' Penny asked. 'What's going to happen to us now, Richard?'

'I have no idea,' I answered gloomily.

Sharifia — under arrest

The Sharifia, the Jeddah police headquarters, was a drab two-storey building. It looked as if it dated back to the days of the Turkish occupation, and the nineteenth century. Plaster was flaking off its grubby white walls. Small sections were crumbling away. Taking up no more than about half an hectare in all, it was surrounded by a high wall capped with halves of broken bottles.

Around the perimeter of its sandy courtyard stood three or four cells with small barred windows and forbidding steel doors. In one corner was the stinking toilet block. A few straggly palm trees broke up the scene.

Penny and I were herded into the down-at-heel yard by policemen armed with semi-automatic rifles that glinted in the sun. We waited anxiously in the heat for the others who had been at the party to be hauled in from the port area.

The party had been Penny's idea.

And it was Helen Smith who discovered the reason for the party.

'You'll never believe this but I've just met someone who is the spitting image of my brother,' Helen enthused one day. 'He's absolutely super.'

I looked up from the paperwork on my desk at the Bakhsh Hospital where we both worked. 'Oh yes? So who is this super fellow?'

'His name's Tim Hayter, and he's from New Zealand. He's a salvage diver and he's going to teach me how to scuba dive. He's ever so interesting.'

'Mmm, I'd like to meet him.' I wanted to learn scuba diving myself.

Tim lived on a barge at the port with a dozen or so German marine workers who were clearing away the many wrecks that lay in Jeddah Harbour. Most of his German colleagues, who were employed by the Harms Salvage Company, did not speak much English. So Tim was pleased to meet English people.

A tall strongly built man with blond hair and piercing blue eyes, he was in his early thirties and cut a handsome figure. His jovial personality ensured him many friends and, I gathered, many girl friends.

'Tim's going on leave for a few weeks. Let's hold a farewell party for him,' said Penny one day, eager for any distraction to her regimented life in Jeddah.

'Tim? Tim Hayter? Why do we need to give a party for him? Can't he throw his own party?' I replied distractedly, my thoughts still at the Bakhsh Hospital and a problem patient's particularly taxing medical condition.

'No, of course he can't. You know he lives on a barge in the harbour.'

Penny was right. Tim lived in a secure area where entry passes were required. We had visited him there for the first time just a few days earlier and experienced for ourselves the rigid security and the difficulty in obtaining permits to enter the area.

It made sense to hold the party in our flat. I agreed halfheartedly to Penny's suggestion, and thought no more about it. My life and my job at the hospital seemed far more important than the details of a minor get-together.

The other late-staying guest ensnared by events at the party was Jacques Texier, a big, burly Frenchman. A freelance diver who did contract work for the Harms Salvage Company, Jacques spoke excellent English. He had lived in the Far East for most of his life and fought at Dien Bien Phu with the French Foreign Legion. Jacques lived on a Greek caique moored in Obhor Creek, a sort of recreational area, a few miles north of the city. Jacques had modified the large wooden fishing boat and installed a compressor to make it a useful dive vessel.

Jacques came to the party to pay Tim some money he owed him for a marine battery.

◫◫◫

Now the four of us were locked in police custody, waiting for the remaining party guests to be brought in for questioning.

'I've drunk lots of water, Richard.'

'Good.'

'What's taking so long? I hope this is over soon.'

'So do I, Penny. So do I.'

The others arrived about an hour later: Martin Fleischer; Harry Goodside, Jeddah boss of Harms; Manfred Schlafer, diver; Klaus Ritter, Harms company cook; and Dieter Chapuis, Harms marine engineer.

All of us were soon bundled into three police Toyota Land Cruisers. Under armed guard, we were driven directly to the general hospital for blood tests. The issue of alcohol consumption was beginning to loom larger than that of the two deaths, I realised in panic.

Trying to suppress my anxiety, I deliberately turned my attention to the surroundings and the proceedings. If I could concentrate on these, I could contain my fear.

I looked closely at the general hospital.

Until now, I had been accustomed to the comparatively modern conditions of the Bakhsh private hospital. Constructed in modules in the United States, shipped out to Saudi Arabia and bolted together like huge building blocks, the Bakhsh Hospital was a piece of modern civilisation dropped into the desert.

The Bab Sharif was no such hospital. It was an unkempt concrete structure. The reception area was full of locals, who squatted on the floor as they waited for a doctor. The smell of decaying garbage permeated the corridors through which we were led.

'Wait here.'

Our group was left in a small room. Before we had a chance to question one another, the door opened and a short hospital orderly, looking all of fourteen years old, came in. I watched as he prepared his equipment. Eventually, he asked Martin Fleischer to prepare his arm. He, this child, was to take our blood samples. Not if I had anything to do with it; I did not trust the skills of such a youngster.

'Here, let me help you,' I offered with a smile. While he looked at me in consternation, I took the syringe from his hand and gently slid the needle into one of Martin's veins. As Martin unclenched his fist, I slowly drew out sufficient blood for a sample to be tested for the presence of alcohol. The young technician watched as I repeated the process with the others. Then I let him draw blood from my own arm.

When we returned to the police station, the Dutch consul had arrived, obviously called in over the death of Johannes Otten, a fellow countryman. The consul left shortly afterwards, but we were held for questioning.

'Be absolutely straightforward with all the details,' Dr Bakhsh had advised. As if I had any intention of being otherwise.

'Only the alcohol is of consequence,' he had emphasised, to my further surprise. 'But that should not be a major factor.'

Only the alcohol? What of the deaths? Were those of no concern?

'The investigation may last a few hours but only that,' Dr Bakhsh assured me. A few hours? Why should it take that long?

Suddenly, what was in my mind a straightforward yet tragic accident was proving to be much more complex. It turned out later, of course, that the main problem was that our flat was too tidy. To the authorities this suggested that we were hiding something, which of course we were – the alcohol.

Another difficulty was that of Johannes Otten's missing trousers. His passport had been found in the road some distance away, but the trousers were still missing, and his wallet was never found. Much was made of this curious fact. It raised suspicion; but of what? I had no idea.

Tim Hayter, Penny and I were questioned. Why didn't they let us go after that? We had told them all we knew. We had spoken the truth. We had nothing to hide. Or so I thought.

Jacques Texier was interrogated for two hours. And then, for some reason, he was released. He immediately went to the French Embassy. From there he got a lift to his boat on Obhor Creek.

Later in the day, Francis Geere, the British consul arrived. A tall, serious, bespectacled fellow, he spoke in clipped British tones. Francis seemed to be completely in command of the situation. 'Don't worry about a thing,' he told me, sensing my exasperation. Yet his visit, rather than providing comfort, completely unnerved us.

We remained in the office while Francis spoke with the police chief, who reclined with his feet up on his desk. The plaster walls of the scruffy room were painted a pale glossy green. Cigarette butts and scraps of paper littered the floor. A lounge chair sat against the back wall, its dark green plastic pitted with cigarette burns.

'I'd like a personal guarantee that torture and physical violence will not be used in the case of the British prisoners,' Geere declared matter-of-factly. I gulped. Torture and physical violence? What was in store for us?

'When may I go back to the hospital?' I asked, suddenly gripped with panic.

The police chief looked at me coldly. I was interrupting the procedures.

'You must stay here,' he said.

'Yes, but for how long? When may I go back to the hospital?' I repeated.

'One day, maybe two,' he replied vaguely.

Why did I not believe him?

We were led back into the yard to wait some more. An American named Richard, who was also being held on an alcohol charge, sat there reading a book, which turned out to be *Midnight Express*.

The police station yard, shaded by its few bedraggled palm trees, was mostly sand. By now it was the hottest part of the day and the Arabian summer sun was beating down mercilessly. We took turns sitting on a dilapidated wooden bench, frequently moving it from spot to spot, following the splotches of shade. The 45-degree heat was draining. As well, despondency lay like a great heavy sack on our shoulders.

The idea of escaping did occur to us, but the presence of guards, however listless they appeared, ruled out any such action. There were several of them, and they were well armed, with ominous-looking automatic weapons hanging about them. Besides, we still expected, with naive optimism, that we would be held for only a few more hours.

By this stage I had the strong impression that most accusing fingers pointed in my direction. I had undergone longer and more detailed questioning than the others. In the eyes of my interrogators, the flat was mine, and it therefore followed that the party held there was my responsibility. That I had, in reality, been a fairly indifferent bystander at my own party would have been incomprehensible to the hierarchically minded Saudi police. So I decided I had to acquaint myself with the facts as far as possible. I had, after all, been asleep when the dramatic events of the party had occurred.

'Tell me exactly what happened.' I began asking the others in turn, seeking their detailed recollections and mentally noting their responses. Slowly, little by little, I put the pieces together. Until I had, what I thought, was the complete picture.

Much has been made of those few hours, from the evening of Saturday 19 May to the early morning of Sunday 20 May 1979. Millions of words have been written in hundreds of newspapers and magazines, from Australia to Greece, from Russia to Spain, from England to America, from Malaysia to France, from Italy to Holland, starting false rumours, incriminating innocent people and raising doubts and suspicions about what was in fact a mundane, even tedious, social gathering. Accounts of sex orgies and mysterious Arab visitors, murder conspiracies and even CIA and British Intelligence involvement have circulated.

The party, or more accurately its tragic aftermath, has had global notoriety. It effectively destroyed my marriage, devastated my relationship with my children and ruined my surgical career in Saudi Arabia as well as Great Britain.

回彐回

That Saturday evening, 19 May, was intended to be a casual low-key affair. We had extended a general invitation to Tim and his friends from the diving company, and I asked along some of the nurses from the hospital. As it was, Helen was the only one of the nursing staff to take up our invitation.

Saudi Arabia in mid-May is unbearably hot. Indoors, despite the constant whirring of fans and the incessant rattle of air conditioning, one is bathed in sweat. Our sixth floor flat, although smaller than the dump in which we had spent our first three weeks in Jeddah, proved to have the advantage that its clearer, more condensed layout ensured that air circulated freely.

Immediately inside our apartment, number 12, was an alcove area, where we and our visitors left outdoor footwear, in keeping with the Arab custom of discarding shoes and sandals on coming into a dwelling. This area then led into a hall, off which ran a toilet and bathroom, master bedroom, children's bedroom, kitchen and lounge. Around two walls of the lounge room there was a small balcony approached through two doors.

There were only the most basic of furnishings: beds, a lounge suite, a small cupboard, and so on. Penny added warmth and colour to the small accommodation with cushions and ornaments she bought at the *souk* – the market.

Our maid, Gumja, an Ethiopian woman, kept our apartment clean. She took great pride in her work and she used to polish the balcony tiles religiously; they were large, around fifteen centimetres square, sandy red in colour and glazed. Gumja kept them spotless. She rubbed them to such a smooth finish that they glistened and sparkled in the sun. Under hot sweaty feet, they were slippery, and really treacherous. Gumja insisted on maintaining the shiny finish. Every day she pushed aside the cheap, flimsy – and broken – sun-lounger with its light tubular aluminium skeleton, as she toiled on her hands and knees.

The party started without me.

Although I officially finished work at nine o'clock, I did not usually leave until ten or later, after I had made my final ward round. The evening of the party, however, I finished more or less on time and I was walking out of the hospital through the casualty department when I spotted Helen, still on duty.

'Are you coming to the party?' I asked.

'Yes. I've almost finished my shift. Then I'll change out of my uniform and be straight over,' she replied.

I made my way back to the flat alone. Penny met me at the door.

'Thank goodness you're here,' she said, 'we haven't any ice. You'll need to go back to the hospital and get some.'

'Have the guests arrived?'

'Yes. They've been here since half past eight.'

So I turned around and walked straight back to the hospital, and down to the ice machine in the basement. On my way back with the ice, I ran into Helen again. She was leaving the nurses' accommodation block. Over her clothes, she had thrown the ankle length black *abaya* which even Western women need to wear when they leave their residence.

'Who's coming to the party?' Helen asked.

'I don't know. We asked Tim to bring some of his friends so there should be a few new faces.'

We climbed the six flights of stairs together and, as we approached the door of the flat, we could easily hear the strains of Fleetwood Mac.

'Are you sure the music isn't too loud?' I asked Penny on entering.

'Oh it's fine, Richard. Don't make a fuss.'

'I'm not. But you know how poor the insulation is and I don't want Ian grumbling again.' Dr Ian Keith, anaesthetist at the Bakhsh Hospital, lived on the floor below with his wife and two children. For some reason the two of us had not hit it off – there used often to be slight rancour between anaesthetists and surgeons, maybe because of the disparity of pay scales. In this case, our poor relationship was strained further by complaints about the noise level in our flat.

'Relax, Richard. Just calm down and enjoy yourself.' Then, turning to Helen, Penny greeted her with a smile. 'Come through and meet everyone.'

I slipped off my shoes and Helen her sandals, and placed them in the alcove with the other footwear already there.

I went ahead, leaving Helen to take off her *abaya*. She followed me into the lounge area moments later. She was wearing a pastel pink dress covered with floral patterns.

Looking around the room, I searched for people I knew. First I greeted Alan. At twenty-five pounds sterling a bottle, I hoped the dozen bottles of whisky I had bought from him would last for a while. As well as the whisky, we had the usual Jeddah assortment of grog available that night: some gin the Harms people had made in their illicit still, and the last of some home-made wine I had brewed several weeks before.

Martin Fleischer, who had visited our flat a couple of days ago with Helen, was another face I knew. But, in the main I saw unfamiliar faces. They appeared to be Tim's friends and workmates. I poured myself out a whisky and added a few chunks of ice.

'Richard, how are you?' It was Tim. 'Have you recovered from yesterday's dive?' he laughed.

'Just about. It's lucky I don't get seasick,' I responded, referring to the fact that the sea had been very rough.

Tim introduced me to his work colleagues. One was Johannes

Otten, the Harms Salvage Company's tug boat captain. Johannes was a tall, heavily built Dutchman, about 182 centimetres tall. I found him a delightful fellow, very open, a gifted conversationalist; he spoke excellent English and had led an interesting life, travelling far and wide in his years at sea.

The glasses he wore gave him a studious air, but he smiled a lot and the spectacles did not detract from his good looks. I noticed Helen glancing in his direction and was not surprised, later on that night, to see them dancing closely together.

Penny and Helen were popular dance partners that night, there being no other women present and even I felt relaxed enough to dance. But, for the most part, I preferred to talk to our guests.

I was watching my intake of whisky, as I was due to perform two operations the following day. At half past eleven I went to tell Penny I was off to do my final ward round of the night.

'See whether you can find some more female guests. Helen and I are feeling a bit outnumbered,' she said.

Outside, it was a relief to be in the cooler air and away from the noise. I strolled down the road to the Bakhsh Hospital where I attended to my post-operative patients and checked up on the two pre-operative ones. The visit took approximately three-quarters of an hour.

As I walked through the quiet streets that night, I began to feel drawn by the exotic charm of Jeddah, the main city of the Hijaz, the Western Region of Saudi Arabia that flanks the Red Sea. Its location makes Jeddah the gateway to the holy cities of Islam. For more than a thousand years, pilgrims from the far flung Muslim world assembled in Jeddah before setting out on the eighty-kilometre trek across the desert to Mecca, the birthplace of their faith. Most of them made their way to Jeddah by camel. Others spent years walking across Africa, from as far away as Nigeria, to Cairo or the Red Sea ports of Egypt and Sudan. From the fifteenth century until World War I, Jeddah and the Hijaz were loosely controlled by the Turkish Ottoman Empire.

After the opening of the Suez Canal, Jeddah became even more important. Muslims from the Eastern Mediterranean, and North Africa made the journey by sea, rather than across the perilous deserts, and Jeddah became the port of entry from all points of the globe.

Before we went there, I had a mind's eye picture of Jeddah as it used to be at the beginning of the twentieth century. I remembered Peter O'Toole as Lawrence capturing the seedy little town of Akaba when he and the soldiers of Sharif Husain swept away the remnant Ottoman imperial army.

Until the middle of the twentieth century, hiring donkeys and tents to pilgrims was the main source of income for the ruling families of the Hijaz. Then Saudi Arabia became the world's largest oil producer, and Jeddah transformed itself into the commercial capital of one of the wealthiest countries in the world.

If Penny and I expected to find in Jeddah traces of the romance of old Araby, we were soon disillusioned. The new city was quite a shock. The town rose abruptly from the brown, sandy wastes of the surrounding desert. At first glance, not a blade of grass was to be seen. It all looked haphazard, unplanned. The centre of the city was a nightmare of holes, partly finished buildings and unpaved, winding lanes. Everything looked raw to us. There were plenty of elegant-looking, modern skyscrapers, but they rose out of rubble and unmade streets. Jeddah looked like a building site. Half-finished tower blocks were fringed by jumbles of breeze blocks, reinforcing rods and sand heaps. There was a pall of dust; Jeddah was hot, dirty and smelly. Thankfully the humidity was low. There was the constant din of car horns, and five times a day calls to prayer were transmitted by giant loudspeakers.

Despite it all, I decided I couldn't complain; we had after all come by choice to a developing city, and an Islamic one at that. We had made a lot of interesting friends, Arab as well as expatriate, and tonight's party seemed to be going well. Certainly, that night, I felt good about our life in Saudi Arabia.

Before going home again, I called on Agnes Johnstone, the hospital matron. I intended to invite her to the party. I knocked on her door but there was no answer, so I went on back to the flat.

On my return, about thirty minutes after midnight, the party was much as before except that the music was louder, and the guests appeared to be slightly more merry. Bodies were swaying to the rhythms of Wings and Captain and Tenille. Klaus, the Harms company cook, in particular, was enjoying himself. His fat bulk leant one way, then another as he grinned away, to no one in particular and announced, 'I'm having a wonderful time.' He told me briefly over the din about his life before Jeddah. Starting work as a builder, he went to sea on a fishing boat at the age of eighteen. The cook fell overboard, so Klaus took over the job. He joined a bigger boat as the second cook, and only then attended cooking school. After that he worked for thirteen years on a big tug. He nearly started two restaurants in Germany but was diddled each time.

I, too, became intoxicated with the good atmosphere and, after another couple of whiskies, brought out my camera and snapped a few candid shots.

At two o'clock I decided I had to go to sleep. I knew the party was likely to continue for an hour or two yet so I started to say my goodbyes to the guests and told Penny I was off to bed.

As the evening had progressed, despite the fact that the air conditioner was blasting away, it had become quite hot and sticky in the apartment. I noticed how Helen and Johannes, faces beaming, were now very close, arms entwined as they danced, both sweating profusely in the clammy Red Sea night.

They made a handsome pair.

That was to be my last glimpse of them – alive. A young attractive couple, dancing together closely, body to body, happy and relaxed. They looked to have not a care in the world, a world in which nothing existed for them but the moment.

I will always hold that memory in my mind.

'Please excuse me. I must go to bed as I am operating early tomorrow.'

I gave Helen a peck on the cheek and shook Johannes' hand. 'It has been a pleasure to meet you,' he said.

After I went to bed, the party seems to have continued a rather under-organised affair, much as it had been all night.

Certainly people remembered Helen and Johannes exhibiting signs of unambiguous affection towards one another. Some time after 2.00 a.m. – no one was sure exactly when – the two of them had disappeared, most likely out on to the balcony, though this was pure conjecture. Only Penny had seen them step out on to it.

One of those present remembered that, when the Harms Salvage divers were leaving and Johannes' absence was noted, Penny had opened the French windows and looked out on to the balcony. Finding it empty, she assumed that Helen and Johannes had left the balcony, unobserved, through the other door, to be alone together. At the time, everyone thought that they had probably gone back to Helen's flat. It seems reasonable that most grown men and women would mind their own business at that point.

The Harms divers left Johannes to find his own way back when he was ready. They were not abandoning him. Johannes was not one of the group of German nationals. He had worked with them as a tug boat captain, but he was Dutch and an acquaintance, rather than a part of the group. The Germans felt no particular responsibility for him.

As soon as my head hit the pillow, I fell into a deep sleep. I remember nothing until the next morning, when Penny shook me to wake me up.

Something terrible had indeed happened.

回리回

In the police station compound, the day passed slowly. It was obvious the police were not prepared for our continued presence.

Penny was left with us men in the yard for the whole of the day and well into the night. During the afternoon, the chief of police discovered that Jacques had been released. He flew into a rage at the news, and ordered that Jacques be found and brought back.

The day wore on. Tired – we had all had only a few hours' sleep – hungry – we had not eaten all day – thirsty – we had only been sustained with small amounts of water – we became restless and irritable. Eventually a man in typical peasant attire of long, flowing *thobe* and red checkered head dress, presented himself and offered to shop for us. We watched as he disappeared through the gates, towards a local cafe and then returned with bread, fried chicken and Coca-Cola, for which he charged us an exorbitant amount of money. We were in no position to argue.

Impatiently tearing off pieces of chicken and bread, we ate with relish, savouring the welcome meal and giving it a great deal more appreciation than its culinary quality probably deserved.

More interrogations followed. The sessions continued well into the night and through to the early hours of the morning. In the stillness of those dark hours, we were given two thin and well-worn mattresses. They were only a gesture.

Nobody could call me, at 198 centimetres, and with a decent covering of flesh, a small man. The Germans were a reasonably bulky lot too, with Klaus, the cook, quite obese. Two mattresses between eight men and a woman?

Add to that equation the Arab attitude towards male/female contact. Penny would not have been expected to share her mattress with anyone but myself. That left one mattress for six decently sized men and one corpulent character. Feeling quite dismal, we sat on the mattresses, in a corner of the yard, and a few of us attempted to get some semblance of sleep.

At about four in the morning, the Saudi police realised that by their standards detaining a woman in the company of eight men was improper. There being no facilities for women at the police station, they had to take Penny to Ruwais prison. I remember Penny's face taut with fear as she was led away, and my own feeling of helplessness.

Some time later, we were suddenly roused from our uncomfortable sleep and brusquely ordered into two small cells; Jacques Texier, Dieter Chapuis, Klaus Ritter, Martin Fleischer and myself to one, and Tim Hayter, Harry Goodside and Manfred Schlafer into the other.

One day I was a senior surgeon in the city of Jeddah's newest private hospital; on a good salary, living in a comfortable flat, wining and dining with dignitaries and diplomats. Here I was a day later, imprisoned, lying on a bare earth floor near an open cesspit, sleepless, and with no idea of what was going to happen next.

But this was no nightmare, no bad dream from which I would awaken, shuddering in relief. This was the real world. I was in a cell. The door was made of solid steel. The only ventilation came through a small barred opening high up in one wall.

The term 'cell' is too generous. It was more like a little box. The earth floor was covered with hundreds of scuttling cockroaches. I have already described the so-called bedding. The metal roof that made the cell extremely hot, was so low that I could not stand up straight. There was little more than one and a half metres from the iron ceiling to the dusty earthen floor. Apart from the few old blankets it was covered with cockroaches that plied between us and the stinking open toilet. With the daytime temperature in the mid-forties, it was hot as hell, an absolute sweatbox. The hole in the ground that posed as the toilet was a stinking orifice coated with faeces. For water, there was one tap – outside, next to the toilet.

The walls were made of large concrete blocks. The thick metal door was impenetrable and the one tiny window, no larger than thirty centimetres square, had no glass, just metal bars, and was so small that it provided barely any light at all.

Into this cubicle that measured a mere three metres by two, were crammed Martin, Klaus and Dieter, two Arabs there for speeding offences, the American *Midnight Express* reader, and me.

Unreasonably as it turned out, I envied Tim, Harry and Manfred for what I imagined was the greater comfort of their larger cell with its overhead fan. The police made a point of keeping our two groups separate, presumably to prevent us from discussing and exchanging ideas. In other words, I think they kept us apart, in two cells, to stop us trying to collude and to match stories with each other. As if we thought we needed to.

After the sun went down we were left in utter darkness. Luckily, the Harms Salvage Company, employer of my German fellow inmates, soon provided a battery lantern that illuminated our cells.

The day after our arrest, Monday, one of Dr Bakhsh's hospital employees came down. 'Do you need anything?' he asked.

'My diary,' I said, 'and a pen.'

Even at that early stage I realised the importance of recording everything. 'Please tell Dr Bakhsh that we are going to have to stay here for a day or two.'

And that was that. After returning with the things I needed, neither he nor Dr Bakhsh made further contact.

From that day, though, I had something in which to make notes. Opening the small Arabic diary with its green plastic cover and with the dates running, by our reckoning, from the back of the book to the front, I first scribbled down what I knew of the chain of events on the evening of Saturday 19 May 1979. I recorded all the details I remembered of the party while they were still fresh in my mind.

Some time after I finished writing, I was sitting on a bench in the courtyard with the rest of the group, making the most of the scraps of time we were allowed out of the cells. Nearby, palm trees rustled in the slight breeze.

'Daddy, Daddy.' I looked up to see William and Lucy running towards me and giggling with excitement. Their short visit, lasting no more than twenty minutes, was an unexpected surprise, joy and boost to me. They chattered away, telling me what fun they were having staying with our friends Keith and Judy Hindle. Then their mood changed.

'When are you coming home, Daddy?' William asked earnestly.

'Soon,' I promised, 'very soon.'

'Can we have a present when you get out?' asked Lucy.

'Yes, a big present,' pleaded William.

'A present? Of course you shall have a present. You'll have lots of presents,' I laughed.

Penny's visit, later that day, was a different matter. 'The prison is dreadful,' she told me tearfully. 'The police keep eyeing me up and they jostle me every chance they get. And the press knows all about us, Richard. There has been a front-page article in the *Daily Mail*.'

I was stunned. An article in a British newspaper? So soon? Were we news? And front page news at that?

'Maybe it will help,' I mumbled, 'maybe the publicity will help to get us out of here quickly.'

◻◿◻

Within a few days in the police cells, I settled into my situation. One adjusts quickly, and starts making a life. My initial feelings of fear and panic had given way to a calm acceptance and my early revulsion at our living conditions was starting to, if not fade, at least turn to tolerance. In my small group, spirits were fairly good. Not so the others.

My assessment of their situation could not have been more wrong. 'There are nineteen of us in here, can you believe it?' Tim Hayter told me through the bars. Nineteen men in a cell no larger than three metres by four. The overhead fan would not make much difference.

Each morning, we woke with the sun, between 5.30 and 6.00. The heat was oppressive by 9.00. Days passed slowly, with reading, interspersed with eating meals, and by 6.30 it was dark. We went to sleep soon after 8.00.

There were no formal meals as such; the police provided only minimal supplies. Like other prisoners, we were expected to rely on our own resources to get by. We lived on food provided by Harms Salvage or bought for us from a nearby shop, with our own money by the guards; chicken and rice, soft drinks and tea. The hospital sent down some food to us now and again. We really depended on the food supplied by the German company, a huge Esky of food that was delivered daily.

The food was adequate, but the hygiene situation was not. Water was scarce, and we washed standing up. When I finally felt compelled to clean out the filthy, stinking toilet, stripped to the waist and up to my armpit down the shit-hole, I found a shoe, belt, and wallet inside it.

We whiled away the long hours reading books and magazines also provided by Harms Salvage who even sent another mattress, so now three of us could sleep a little more comfortably. We stopped talking about the party – there was nothing more to say – or about the fix we were in – there was nothing we could do about that, except wait.

We read. We chatted a little. We slept. It was hot as hell, coming up to mid-summer and the noon temperature was obviously in the mid-forties most days. With the metal roof over us, it was suffocating.

Once a day, we were allowed out of the cell, mainly during the evening. We just wandered around in the small dusty yard, grateful for the smallest amount of exercise, the shortest escape from our stifling confines.

Hopes were raised. On the Wednesday, we were given the impression we would be released by the following Monday. Just four more days to wait. But Monday came and went with no change in our situation. Early on, my own moods fluctuated. I recall feeling almost cheerful one evening, and indifferent to whatever might happen to us. It seemed clear to me that Penny and I must separate. But the following day, after a bad night spent tossing and turning in the sultry heat, I felt a heavy hand bear down on me; and what had seemed clear only a few hours before was now muddled and confused. Visitors came and went – embassy officials with no news, hospital bureaucrats without fresh information, British expatriate friends bearing articles from the British press. Dreadful, sensational, I felt when I read them. These will not help us at all. And, indeed, the publicity aggravated our predicament.

Encouragement came in the form of letters and visits. 'What does not kill me, makes me stronger,' Klaus read to me from a letter he received from Harms Salvage, his employers. 'What does not kill me, makes me stronger.' Those words of Nietzsche gave me comfort and sustained me over the next months. That maxim became my anthem.

'Harms also say this could have happened to anyone,' Klaus added. 'We were just the unfortunate ones.' The unfortunate ones indeed.

And all along, one thought kept pulsating through my mind. Why were we being held? For what reason? On what grounds? No one could tell me anything. I was advised to be patient. And wait. And keep on waiting. One by one, we were interrogated repeatedly by the police. These sessions took place late at night and carried on until the early hours of the morning. I gained the impression that the police had no doubt the two deaths were accidental. So why were we still being held?

Snippets of information came from unexpected sources.

'What time did Helen Smith and Johannes Otten die?' the police asked me in one bout of questioning.

'I don't know,' I replied, 'some time between 2.30 and 5.30 a.m., I believe.'

'We know exactly when they died. At 3.15 a.m.,' one of them told me.

'How do you know that?'

'By the time on Johannes Otten's watch.'

回己回

'Look, this will blow over quickly and you will soon all be out,' British consul, Francis Geere told us on one of his visits. But no progress seemed to be made. Finally, he admitted 'it's going to take a bit longer'.

How long was 'a bit longer'? I thought, once we had given our statements and been interviewed, that would have been it. Surely the fact that we were all saying the same things, without having had a chance to concoct any sort of a story, would convince our interrogators that we were telling the truth.

It turned out that a bit longer was going to mean a lot longer. Instead of the few hours they had first estimated, the British Embassy, and Francis Geere, now informed us that sorting out this matter might take as long as three or four months.

By then, we had been held in the prison cells for nine days. Confined inside for much of the time, our group was restless. Dieter complained continually at the lack of exercise. Penny was brought over for a visit. She looked drawn. She had been left for nearly twelve hours without food. Meanwhile I had other matters to concern me.

While I was being cross-examined yet again, the door of the main office burst open. An irate Saudi civilian dragged in a workman, using as a noose the rope from the man's *gutra* or headpiece. He was half strangling his victim. Shouting and screaming, pulling him across the floor, he was obviously accusing the man of some dreadful crime. It turned out this was his employee, an Egyptian labourer. The Egyptian man was being accused of stealing, a charge he vigorously denied.

Later that day, I watched through the tiny cell window, as the Egyptian was dragged out into the yard. Two policemen put a rope around a piece of wood and wrapped it around his feet, twisting tighter and tighter. One policeman held up each end while others took it in turn to beat the bare soles of his feet with heavy canes.

Whack, whack, whack.

The canes slashed swiftly through the air and the man's screams of pain were bloodcurdling. I listened to the victim's pleas for mercy. Dear God, let them stop beating him and let us be spared from a similar torment.

The policemen beat their victim's feet until he fainted in agony. They threw a bucket of cold water over him and brought him round. Time after time they repeated the process, beating him to unconsciousness and then reviving him to endure more suffering.

The policemen beat the Egyptian's feet to an absolute pulp. Blood was pouring everywhere. They must have broken every bone. He could no longer walk. He could not even hobble on the bloodied mass as they dragged him away.

Not content with that torture, the following day the police began again, this time with a kind of crucifixion. The Egyptian was suspended from the branch of a tree by a rope through his handcuffs so that the tips of his battered toes barely touched the ground. There he remained for some hours in the stinking heat, supporting his weight with his feet as best he could and, when the pain became unbearable, just hanging by his wrists.

The lethal aspect of this and its similarity to Biblical crucifixion lies in the fact that in this position the victim slowly suffocates because he is unable to breathe adequately. Then, as the blood pressure drops due to blood pooling in the veins of his unsupported legs, blood supply to the brain falls below a critical level. The oxygen level in the brain drops; unconsciousness occurs and death slowly follows.

The poor fellow was groaning and moaning and fainting. But, as on the day before, the police kept reviving him with buckets of cold water. The episode was hideous. And again, it was happening just outside our cell. Was this demonstration of police brutality being put on for our benefit, I wondered? If so, it terrified me. Was this the torture to which Francis Geere had been alluding, the first time he visited us?

Finally the man groaned again, fell unconscious but was ignored. I could not stand it.

'*Areef, areef!*' I bellowed. 'Guard, guard, cut him down! Cut him down!'

I continued yelling until the guard called his superior.

'Cut him down, cut him down at once!' I repeated.

The two of them stared at me blankly. Then they cut him down and dragged him away.

I never saw him again.

The tension built up for a few more days. Then the Saudi detective in charge of the case, a cluey sort of bloke called Samir who had spent some time in England and hence spoke good English, confided in me, 'I am satisfied there was no foul play in the two deaths.'

At last. Finally this would all be over.

'But there are other matters.'

'What matters?' I asked.

'The alcohol.'

I gulped. It was just as I had thought. The alcohol would be a problem. And to think that we had gone to all the trouble of disposing of it, only to confess to serving it at the party. Now the alcohol was to be our downfall.

'It was also a mixed party,' he added. Much was being made of men and women having been in the same area. Under Saudi law that was forbidden for all but members of the same family. Even at family get-togethers, women tended to remain apart from men, socialising in different rooms.

Until then, I had not been particularly frightened. I had been more concerned about the time it was all taking. Things were serious but I didn't believe there was a great deal to worry about. We were merely being held for a short time for questioning. At worst, I might end up carrying the can for the party, which took place in my flat and at which there was alcohol. But no great feeling of terror possessed me.

Now it seemed, all of a sudden, matters were not so straightforward. From that day on, with police and later on, lawyers, even at the sharia court, the Muslim religious court, no mention was made of murder or attempted murder. It was accepted by everyone that the deaths of Helen Smith and Johannes Otten were accidental. Nevertheless, there was a problem, a large social problem, which as far as the Saudi authorities were concerned, was a big crime.

On his next visit, Francis Geere took me aside for more good news. 'I've spoken to the chief of police of the Western Region,' he told me. 'He says you will definitely get prison sentences.'

This was all too horrifying. What could we do? There seemed to be no help for us from any quarter. In desperation, I even thought of contacting a princess of the royal house who had been a patient of mine. As one of the daughters of the late King Abdul Aziz, perhaps she could mediate on our behalf. I had visions of her sweeping in and commanding: 'Release this doctor and these people immediately.'

We were interviewed time and again over the next few days. The questions were always the same. Where had the alcohol come from? What had people drunk? How much had they drunk? The police wanted to know at what times people had arrived and left. They wanted to know how well we had known Helen and whether Martin and Tim were interested in her. Was there any suggestion of jealousy? Had the police conjured up some sort of love triangle, I wondered. Their questions were always the same and our answers were always the same. We seemed to be getting nowhere. What was the sticking point? Why were we not released?

Finally, Samir, the Saudi chief investigator, told me, 'We are worried about this. We think Penelope and Tim are holding something back.'

I looked puzzled.

'We don't think they are telling us the truth,' he continued.

'I'm sure they are telling you the truth,' I replied. 'None of us has anything to hide. We don't know anything more. We have told you everything.'

'No, no, we are sure they are not telling us the truth,' he insisted. 'In my opinion, there is more to this, and Penelope and Tim hold the key.'

One evening soon after that, Klaus Ritter was interviewed. He seemed to be away for a long time. 'The police think Tim and Penny are holding something back,' he told us when he arrived back in the cell.

I was perplexed. Was it what the detective had been warning me about? I was also wary. With our group separated into two cells, I wondered whether the police were trying to set us against each other. Were they telling one group something and then waiting for a response from the other? But there seemed to be some omen in what Klaus was saying.

My first inkling of the truth came shortly after, when the Harms Salvage managing director arrived from Europe. During his visit with his men in my cell, I picked up three words in their conversation: 'Tim . . . *geschlafen* . . . Penny.'

Who could I discuss this piece of news with? Tim was in the other cell, Penny was away at the women's prison and I was too embarrassed to attempt to question my German cellmates. The answer would have to wait.

Helen's Father

Somewhere in my mind, I must have known that what appeared to be a straightforward yet tragic accident would not be dealt with swiftly. And that led me to keep a diary of events to use during any future inquiry. My first meeting with Helen's father justified my faith in my diary.

Ron Smith had flown out to Saudi Arabia from England soon after hearing of his daughter's death. The Saudi police were excited to have a 'British policeman' in their midst. Ron Smith, perhaps inadvertently, left them with the impression he was a senior detective connected with Scotland Yard. A Yorkshireman, with the characteristic, broad accent of that county, his blunt talk and brusque manner soon began to exasperate Saudi officials.

At any rate, he wanted to talk to us, and to me in particular. I first met him on 26 May, less than a week after the tragedy. I wanted to talk with him as I thought of how I would feel at the death of a daughter. I wanted to express my sympathy. I was told he had been divorced just the week before. 'The poor man must be cut to ribbons', I later noted in my diary.

Ron Smith was ushered in to the Sharifia police station courtyard. The morning breeze provided a slight relief from the overpowering heat. We sat together on a wooden bench. Nearby a guard, his green uniform faded by the sun and his boots scuffed by the sand, sat on a chair, cradling his semi-automatic. He glanced over at us occasionally, and spat frequently into the dirt. He was coming to the end of his shift and was probably bored and hungry.

Ron Smith was alert and eager for information. A small and slightly built man with wispy hair, he was dressed in a baggy dark suit and tie. Looking haggard and unshaven, his face was sad and drawn. In the blistering heat, and despite the breeze, sweat soon began pouring down his face. He dabbed at it frequently with a large white handkerchief.

I first reacted to Ron Smith as to a grieving parent. I tried to console and reassure him. I spoke to him as I would to the parents of a patient who had died. I attempted to comfort him and perhaps assuage his grief.

I told him how Helen had been a popular young woman, an outgoing and bubbly girl with a good sense of humour. She had been well liked by the rest of the hospital staff. I described to him the events of the party and its consequences. I told him how the balcony railing had only been eighty or so centimetres in height, and emphasised how easily two people could have toppled over, especially at night and if intoxicated.

I told him quite freely what I had told the police. In return, Ron Smith just muttered. He did not comment much, if at all. He sat, turned slightly away from me, and fiddled frequently with his right coat pocket. A niggling unease grew in my mind as I spoke to him. The tension was exacerbated by Ron Smith's apparent restlessness.

It puzzled me that he was here at all. For Helen had led us to believe that she and her father were not particularly close. I recall that she had nominated her mother, not her father, as 'next of kin' in her passport.

She spoke freely about her brothers and her mother – but I could recall only very rare occasions when she mentioned her father. Although Helen remained close to her mother and siblings, father and daughter had had little or no contact for seven years. And Helen's wandering took her as far as Jeddah, in Saudi Arabia.

◙꙰◙

I first met Helen Smith while she was sitting in a Bakhsh Hospital office with some of the other nurses. They were bored and passing the time until the hospital opened officially and their work began. They were desperate for something to do. There were as yet few tasks around the hospital.

The nurses were housed in a block of eight flats. The nurses' quarters were crowded, with two or three to a small room. As unaccompanied women, they had little opportunity to get out and visit the Old Town with its glittering *souk* or to swim in the Red Sea, with its sandy beaches, warm blue water and beautiful coral reefs teeming with multicoloured fish. Any diversion was welcome. Even something as humdrum as helping with housework or babysitting was a refreshing change.

'I'm looking for someone to give my wife a hand with the ironing,' I said to the nurses. 'Is anyone interested?' Helen leapt at the chance and with that mundane start there began our friendship with Helen Smith. She was just twenty-two years old. A dark-haired woman of medium height, she had an attractive face, a warm ready smile and a vivacious personality.

Over the following weeks, she became a frequent visitor to our flat and I often came home from work to find her in deep discussion with Penny or playing with our children, William and Lucy, who came to adore her.

Helen soon established a busy social life for herself, something few of the other nurses achieved. She had a string of admirers who made great demands on her free evenings. But if ever we found her in, she was always a willing babysitter, much to the delight of the children.

Helen never accepted payment for any of this but we gave her presents instead and she brought her washing to do in our machine. When she admired Penny's handbag, we bought her an identical one.

Helen was an open, generous happy-go-lucky sort of girl, full of fun and nonsense. She loved parties and she loved male company. It was no secret that she had a number of Arab boyfriends during her time in Saudi Arabia. They were fairly short-term relationships but she made an impact.

'Look at my beautiful watch,' she said one evening, showing off her latest present.

'It's gorgeous,' agreed Penny.

I was more cautious. 'You'll get yourself into trouble if you carry on like that,' I commented, sounding like an authoritarian parent. For I knew the powers-that-be, had they known, would not have taken kindly to this fraternising with the Jeddah Saudis.

Helen merely laughed. 'Oh no, it's great fun,' she replied.

Behind her bright and cheerful demeanour, I always sensed that Helen was sad at heart. Her fairly brisk love life in Jeddah may have been an attempt to compensate. She apparently displayed her small presents as if to say, 'They really do love me, you know.'

Helen – her happy smiling face, her kindness towards our children, her cheerful personality. It was not often that I saw her unsettled or distraught. One such time was after she developed a strong relationship with a man called Guruswami, a Malaysian cleaner at the hospital. We all called him Guru. He and Helen became great friends. But things got out of hand after Helen was found in Guru's room. Such relationships were forbidden.

'Guru has been sacked. Dr Bakhsh says he will be deported in the next few days,' Helen sobbed. She was distraught. She and Guru were at our flat, having arrived unannounced, both of them in tears.

'How can they do this to us?' she wept. Then her distress turned to anger. 'How dare they,' she ranted. 'They have no right. I'm going to resign. That's what I'll do. I'll resign immediately and join Guru in Malaysia.'

Penny and I were shocked. I don't think they had come to enlist our help, but rather our sympathy and to cry on our shoulder.

Next day I mentioned the situation to Dr Bakhsh. 'I've heard about Guru,' I began. 'There is a chance that we will lose a good nurse, Helen Smith, over this,' I told him.

'I cannot do anything,' he replied, explaining that the matter had been taken out of his hands. He described how security police had discovered Guru visiting Helen's room and vice versa. They had informed Dr Bakhsh that Guru must be dismissed for 'immoral practices'.

Guru was subsequently given his marching orders and placed on the next plane to Malaysia.

The next time I saw Helen, two days later in my office, she was more composed but no less determined.

'I have resigned,' she said.

'Oh, Helen, don't be silly,' I replied. 'How can you possibly think of throwing away your job and your career over this man?'

She hesitated.

'Look, if you really care about him that much, you can always meet up with him afterwards,' I told her, 'when your contract is over.'

She wiped away her tears. 'I suppose so.' But she still sounded unconvinced.

'Don't rush into anything. Just think about it all seriously.'

She remained silent.

'Helen, if Guru's affection for you is as strong as you say, he'll wait. You can re-join him in Malaysia in a few months' time.'

Helen stayed upset for a while but got over the breakup fairly quickly. Soon she was back to her effervescent and gregarious self.

◨◱◨

Now Helen was dead, and her father had suddenly appeared on the scene, in the role of grieving father. Why did Ron Smith come all the way to Jeddah? What was going on in his mind?

I did not have to wait long to find out.

◨◱◨

After that first puzzling meeting with Ron Smith, I returned to the cell drained and exhausted, mostly by the heat. The others — Martin, Klaus and Dieter — were envious that I had been allowed out while they had remained cramped in our dark and dingy stall. The familiar stench from the so-called toilet, that hole in the ground, hit my nostrils again and I felt ill. The heat was uncomfortable enough outside, but unbearably oppressive here. We sweltered. The cockroaches scurried about. I lay down on the thin mattress and closed my eyes. I drifted into a peaceful sleep. I still had hope. Things could be worse.

◨ ꌅ ◧

And, the very next day, they were.

Francis Geere returned with Ron Smith. He was a changed man. The quietly grieving father of the previous afternoon was now a fierce and angry figure.

'You're not telling me the truth,' he yelled. 'There's something wrong, you're covering something up.'

'What do you mean?' I asked in astonishment. 'I told you all I know.'

'You lied,' he spluttered, his complexion growing ruddier by the second. 'You lied and I've got proof,' and he produced a small tape recorder from his pocket, the same pocket with which he had been fiddling the previous day. The recording device had been there all along.

I was taken aback. What on earth had possessed him to do such a thing? And how on earth could he have been so calculating as to have thought of such a thing? There was much more to Ron Smith than met the eye. He was going to make life very difficult.

Ron Smith glared at me, anger in his eyes. 'You told me that your wife, Tim and the others went out on to the balcony to watch the sun rise.' He spat out the words.

'Yes,' I agreed, with some hesitation in my voice. It was not clear what he was driving at.

'That's rubbish,' he hissed, 'absolute rubbish. The sun rises in the other direction.'

'But when I said sunrise, I meant –'

He did not give me time to reply.

'What's more,' and he launched into details of the time of sunrise that day. Somewhere locally, he had researched the exact time.

'You didn't report the deaths to the police immediately. What were you doing in that time?'

I didn't know what to say. When I had said 'sunrise', I had used the term loosely. It would have been more correct to say that Penny, Tim and Jacques were really looking at the dawn light. But it was just a question of semantics, a well-used phrase, 'watching the sun rise'. Unfortunately, a couple of words to which Ron Smith attached great significance. Those two words, casually spoken, were now being taken as evidence of suspicious circumstances, as an affirmation of foul play, a cover-up.

'What were you doing in that time?'

'What time? There was no time. We informed the authorities immediately.'

I sat horrified as Ron Smith continued to berate me about bruises found on Helen's body and the depressed abrasion on her forehead.

'That proves there was foul play,' he bellowed.

'Not at all, what I said was –'

But he cut me off again in mid-sentence. He seemed not the least bit interested in what I had to say.

'You lied to me,' he insisted. 'How can I believe anything you say?'

Ron Smith seemed to have a Jekyll-and-Hyde personality, one day devastated, sad and withdrawn; the next animated and furious.

⊡⊡⊡

All at once, there was movement in our case. But movement we could have done without. Things went from bad to worse. The Saudi police were slightly impressed by Ron Smith for a while, under the misapprehension he had worked with the London Metropolitan Police.

As soon as Helen's father cried, 'There's a discrepancy, there's been a cover-up,' the Saudis redoubled their efforts, anxious not to miss or overlook anything.

Soon enough the Saudis found that rather than being a high-ranking detective, Ron Smith's career was that of a constable in Yorkshire.

Next morning, after I had cooled down a little, I returned to my diary. My first entry I composed as if it were an open letter to Ron Smith.

I wrote:

I was appalled at your obvious disbelief of what I told you in good faith two days ago, discussing our conversation with the police and comparing it with the statement I have given. The fact that you either misheard or misquoted two of the points I mentioned upsets me greatly.

I don't want to disillusion you about Helen. I don't know how well you knew her as she spoke more of her mother than she did of you. But Helen was quite promiscuous in Jeddah. She had many boyfriends and admirers and one of them was even deported back to Malaysia because of his affair with her.

But don't get me wrong. I liked Helen a lot and she was a great friend of our family, visiting my wife three or four times a week, helping to put the children to bed, and babysitting . . .

As I told you two days ago, Helen was in great spirits the night she died and not in the least depressed. Neither was she as drunk as you seemed to imply when we met. The Saudi laboratory tests showed just a trace of alcohol in her body. There is not the remotest possibility of foul play.

We were all extremely good friends. No one at that party would dream of harming her or Johannes in any way.

Wherever she is now, I feel certain that Helen would be extremely upset at what you are doing in trying to dig up further details of what was a tragic accident, but nevertheless, one with a simple explanation.

Helen and Johannes took a crazy risk against a railing which was barely two feet six inches high. You are only making matters worse for her nine friends by your actions.

I urgently suggest that you take Helen's body back to England at the earliest opportunity.

I feel certain that if Helen was aware that she was the cause of several of her close friends going to gaol for up to six months, she would do everything possible to help matters, not make them worse.

◧⛌◨

The Saudi police were still going along with Ron Smith's accusations of foul play and things were beginning to look bleak. The strain continued to build up for a few days until the Saudi detective Samir took me aside, and informed me that the police had now formed the opinion Ron Smith may be grief stricken and that his allegations were baseless.

'We think he is making trouble,' he told me.

I breathed a sigh of relief. At last the truth would come out.

Although Ron Smith had succeeded in stirring up the Saudis at the outset, his allegations had by now been totally discounted by them. Several other Saudi policemen told me, independently, that they had no time for Ron Smith and his stories.

In any event, Ron Smith never had the opportunity to read the contents of my diary, or the open letter I wrote to him. And then, during the evening of 30 May, after eleven days in detention, we were suddenly shackled together and transferred to the main prison of Jeddah.

Ruwais — Jeddah prison

HOW TO PUT ON TROUSERS WHEN WEARING FETTERS
Trousers must be loose fitting. Insert left foot into the left trouser leg. Pull the remainder of trousers up through the fetter on that leg. Then feed the seat and other leg of the trousers down the inside of the fetter on the right leg. Then put the right leg into the trousers and pull trousers up, inside the fetter. Button or zip up the flies.

Handcuffed together, in twos, in a police van, at seven o'clock in the evening of Wednesday, 30 May 1979, our eleventh day of captivity, we were transferred to the dreaded Ruwais prison. I felt like a common criminal.

Ruwais was an austere, forbidding building. Set on about two hectares of ground, and surrounded by a three-metre high white wall it was said to date back to the Turkish occupation and the early twentieth century. Partly mud brick, partly cement block, the prison was predominantly white with, here and there, patches of brown clay.

During my time at the Bakhsh Hospital, I used to drive past Ruwais prison every day. It is on the road between the hospital and the embassy section of town, where we shopped at the large Al Mukhtar mall.

We expatriates had all heard stories of the frightening conditions within those walls; appalling cells, prisoners incarcerated for years on end and, most frightening of all, the final exit – the public beheading of less fortunate inmates.

I remembered how I used to drive quickly past the huge pile of rotting garbage that always lay outside the gaol, constantly being picked over by marauding bands of goats, wild cats and the occasional stray dog. Its smell was foul and spread a long way. Now, as we were driven up to the main gate, both the stench and fear made me recoil.

After descending clumsily from the prison wagon, we were led through a solid metal door and into an office. There, our handcuffs were removed. Rubbing my chafed wrists in relief, I gave my name and the other details required. We still had not been charged with any crime. Nor had we any idea of how long we would be locked up there.

Straight after our arrival, we were taken to the *gawaja* (foreigners) block. Seven of us, everyone except Jacques Texier, were ushered into an already overcrowded cell. The place was so dark it was scarcely possible to see through the gloom. A thick pall of cigarette smoke filled the room. I felt myself panic. How would I survive here with my asthma? The condition had returned with a vengeance and, what's more, my Ventolin puffer had run out.

As my eyes adapted to the low light, I made out the forms of other prisoners. I could not bear to count how many men were crammed into a space measuring no more than five metres by six.

There were about eight wings in the prison which housed some 3000 people, mostly men. The cell blocks radiated out like the spokes of a wheel from a central administrative section. The entire area was surrounded by a high wall, almost three metres high, constructed largely of concrete blocks, and controlled by semi-automatic-toting guards. The women's block was separated from the men's gaol by a five metre wall. The wall had only one doorway, and that was guarded at all times.

One of the blocks in our complex was for political prisoners. They were isolated from the rest of us and we had no contact with them. Another block was for children under the age of twelve. They were held mainly as hostages for older relations wanted for a crime and who had either absconded or could not be located by the police.

A concrete courtyard between two of the blocks was marked out as for a netball court and another, between two of the other blocks, contained the mini market or souk, where inmates could buy clothes, canned food and soft drinks each afternoon.

Those of us who were lucky, and this included all Westerners, lived in cells opening onto a central corridor. The less fortunate lived in the corridor itself. They slept there during the night, exposed to the elements and putting up with dust storms or occasional rain. During the day they had to move out, in order to make room for people to use the corridor.

The cell into which I was put at first held twenty-three men, twenty-three being the total number of sleeping mats that could be fitted on to the floor space. In one corner there was a huge pile of rubber mats that were spread out on the floor at night. Each one of us had a mat and we just slept on that, covered by a sheet. It was so crowded at night that, if one sleeper turned over, everyone had to follow suit. The corner was the better position because you could keep a mattress there along the side. If you didn't have a corner and felt tired during the day you had to lie down on the concrete floor.

No furniture whatsoever was provided. One or two prisoners had either manufactured or obtained cupboards that they nailed on to the wall and used to stow a few personal belongings.

In the prison there were no sinks as such. There was just a concrete trough and a few taps where you could fill a bucket. The nearby toilets were the usual Middle Eastern type, just a hole in the ground. In our block there were four or five of these little cubicles and they were constantly foul with faeces. They would be cleaned out occasionally but, most of the time, the area would be absolutely beyond belief – great lumps of excreta lying everywhere and blocked drains. The stench was terrible.

Each morning I gingerly picked my way through to have a total body wash, filling my bucket with the warm water which came out above room temperature, about 60 degrees Farenheit. To wash with water at that temperature was hardly refreshing, and so we learned to draw a bucket of water in the evening, leave it to cool overnight and then have a wash in the morning. Only by doing that could we avoid prickly heat.

The other thing that helped us cope with the intolerable heat were the huge ceiling fans. They would whirr above us at tremendous speed, day and night, keeping the air circulating. Sweat evaporated quite quickly and we could thereby keep comfortably cool. But the moment the fans stopped I would be literally pouring and dripping with sweat.

It was essential to drink copious amounts of liquid. We never drank the tap water as the drains were so primitive but instead bought water by the bottle.

We lived on the floor, sitting there during the daytime and, at meal times, spreading a sheet on which to place the food. There were no forks, knives or spoons and we ate from communal dishes which were brought every meal time by corridor prisoners. We ate Arab-style, using the right hand only, the left strictly reserved for personal toilet duties. Another aspect of eating with the right hand is that because the penalty for repeated theft is amputation of the left hand, the victim then has to use his right hand for personal washing. This then makes him unclean – unfit to eat with others, and compounds his punishment.

The food provided by the prison was dreadfully monotonous. Breakfast was sickly sweet halwa served with reconstituted milk and vast quantities of sugary black tea. Lunch was boiled rice with boiled chicken, fish or mutton. It was devoid of seasoning. I soon found the bland diet completely nauseating. The evening meal consisted of bread, goat's cheese, more halwa and tea.

What saved most of us was the food sent in to many of the prisoners by their families. In the traditional Arab spirit of sharing in adversity, those with food shared with those who had none. As well, Harms regularly sent in food.

Perhaps it was because our plight was becoming increasingly

serious, maybe it was guilt, or possibly fear that I would hear the story from another source; whatever his reasons, that night Tim Hayter decided to confess to me. He told me what had taken place in the early hours of the morning of 20 May. I sat in silence as he admitted that he and Penny had had sexual intercourse on the night of the party.

Finally everything fell into place; the repeated assertions by the Saudi police that Tim and Penny were holding something back, as well as the gossip I had overheard between the Germans.

I did not know what to think. Drained by the heat, stunned by Tim's confession, incarcerated in prison and surrounded by strangers, I felt as if I was in some soap opera, a sensation exacerbated by the drone of an old television set nearby, blaring out a European Cup soccer match. This had to be some hideous surreal dream.

Then my asthma became so bad I thought I would die. That night was a terrifying one as I gasped for breath, thinking that each gulp would be my last. In the early hours, everything seemed hopeless. I was imprisoned in a dirty, clammy Arab gaol. I had no prospect of release in sight. My lucrative position as surgeon at the Bakhsh Hospital was in jeopardy. My wife was incarcerated in God knows what conditions and our confused and perplexed children were separated from us. Friends and acquaintances who had attended a party at my flat were now languishing in prison. And one of those friends and one of those acquaintances were dead.

In the early hours of 31 May, I lay on my uncomfortable thin rubber mat, longing for the clatter of the air conditioning that had provided at least a measure of relief in our flat, and trying to sort out in my mind what crime I had committed against fate to be in this ignominious position. I was to have plenty of time to contemplate the events of the previous couple of weeks and to search for the fatal flaw in my character.

Those following hours and days passed in a haze of shock and disbelief. I was confused and bewildered. I cut myself off from what was happening around me. From somewhere, I obtained a copy of James Clavell's *Shogun* and immersed myself in its pages. I entered another world, that of sixteenth-century Japan, and so left my nightmare reality for a brisk tale of rival warlords, geishas and a shipwrecked Englishman.

After a couple more days, we were told we were to be moved. We were taken to section 5. It was a smaller wing and much less crowded. The prisoners seemed to be entirely Arabs. They were all very friendly and welcoming. There were only about 165 prisoners in all as compared to the 200 plus of the block we had left. It was hard to keep an exact count as prisoners constantly came and went and one in fact died during our time. The block had been designed for eighty men.

Now our group from the party was split, two to a room. Nevertheless, we could come and go as we pleased and we all ate together. Jacques was transferred to another section. The plan seemed to be to keep Jacques, Tim and Penny apart. The three of them were questioned again that day.

'They concentrated on the time from when we woke up to when we saw the bodies,' Tim told me. 'They're now convinced it's murder.'

I gasped as he continued. 'A post mortem is being carried out today.'

Surely that would dismiss any suggestion of murder, I thought. How, why, could anyone possibly think of murder? We had all co-operated fully as soon as the bodies had been discovered. Surely that proved we were not hiding anything. When the police arrived, there were only three or four of us there and we had fetched the others. Everyone had just volunteered to come. There was no running away.

'Oh, and Richard,' Tim continued, 'we are not to sign anything unless an independent interpreter has vetted it.'

life until the party

Locked up in a squalid gaol, even a blithe optimist might ask, 'What have I done to end up in this mess?' And although I forced myself not to give up hope, my future looked bleak. The Quaker philosophy my mother had gently drummed into me left no room for self-pity. Even so, I could hardly bear to think what lay ahead.

Crusty old gentlemen often insist that a spell in the army would do wonders for the younger generation. I don't know whether or not they are right, but maybe my own months inside those harsh stone walls were what I needed to help me make sense of my life. Looking back, I can see that my time in gaol in Jeddah forced me to mature, perhaps in a way that many men and women never achieve.

A particular and personal irony of my being locked away in an Arab gaol was that I came from a family who had provided missionaries and administrators to the Empire. People like me were not destined to share their existence with families of cockroaches.

In fact, I was probably one of the last people to benefit from the British imperial system in full flower. I went 'out' to South Africa as a child where my family and I led lives of some privilege, with plentiful food, spacious houses, domestic servants, holidays in the sun. We were not arrogant people though, and our standard of life would have been no more than we felt we had earned.

I was born near the town of Street in Somerset just before midnight on 28 March 1941. My father was somewhere in the English Channel that night. He was second lieutenant on a mine sweeper. Its dangerous task was to keep shipping lanes clear of the new German acoustic mines.

After the war, by then a young married man with a family, my father took up employment in an Africa that still had place names like Bechuanaland, Nyasaland, Rhodesia, Tanganyika.

For my first two years at school in Africa I went to a government school in Kimberly and later in Kitwe, in Northern Rhodesia where we lived.

In January 1950, when I reached the age of nine, I was sent away to boarding school; St Andrew's prep at Grahamstown, in South Africa.

I don't remember missing home life much. Nor do I remember school very fondly. Life there seemed to be mostly hard work. I had to study harder than most other boys, because I regarded myself as only an average student, and felt I needed to make the extra effort, to get the results I wanted. As well, for some reason or other, I was not very good at ball games. Being a swot and not much help to anyone at football and cricket probably did not endear me to my fellow students.

Almost certainly the most remarkable aspect of my schooling at Grahamstown, near the foot of the African continent, was the distance I had to travel to get there.

My father worked as an engineer for Anglo-American Mining Corporation, in Northern Rhodesia (now Zambia), near the border with Belgian Congo (now the Democratic Republic of Congo). From where we lived in Kitwe, the train journey was 3000 kilometres long, and took five days. During those five days, we travelled from the near-tropics of central Africa to the gentle Mediterranean climate of Eastern Cape Province on the Indian Ocean.

My mother appeared not to consider such a distance any obstacle for a nine year old; later, my brother Tim made the long trip when he was only seven. We did the trip back and forth every term, six times a year in all.

Apart from the very first time, when I was accompanied by my parents who had to organise such things as my school uniform, I made the journey with only other prep students for company. For all the boys, those five days were an extraordinary hiatus of freedom, between home and school. Most of us smoked prodigiously during the five days of liberty. Our chosen brand was Springbok, which in today's terms would have a high tar rating indeed. I don't recall any of us ever bothering with liquor.

Rhodesian Railways carriages were comfortable, and the food was copious, especially the 'full' breakfast, which was enough to keep a ravenous small boy quiet well into the afternoon. During breakfast one morning, I was entertained by an enraged bull elephant making mock charges at the train, which had in some way offended him.

On our way south we passed over the Tropic of Capricorn. Soon, we crossed the Zambesi River, with a crossing and view of the awesome Victoria Falls.

At Bulawayo we changed into a South African Railways carriage and, after long halts with African dancers and hawkers and street markets at every station, the train made its way across the Kalahari Desert into the idyllic pastures of Eastern Cape Province, and our destination, Grahamstown.

When our three years were up, most of the prep boys from St Andrews, Grahamstown, went on to the senior college of the same name. However, I was lucky enough to win a scholarship to a new school, Peterhouse, near Salisbury (now Harare), Southern Rhodesia (now Zimbabwe). Of course, Salisbury was much closer to home, only 1500 kilometres away. The founder of the new school was Fred Snell, who had left South Africa to avoid the increasingly racist and draconian rule of the Nationalist Party which had been elected in 1948. Fred Snell succeeded in integrating black and white students in his new Peterhouse school. The masters at Peterhouse had been carefully chosen, many of them coming from British schools.

One important sport at Peterhouse, to me anyway, was rock climbing on the granite outcrops called koppies which were so numerous in that part of Rhodesia. It turned out to be a skill which I could use in other countries and in other terrains, and indirectly led to my career as a surgeon.

My deciding to study medicine may have been influenced by my father's cousin, Charles Fisher, who was a surgeon on the copperbelt. Earlier, he had been a missionary surgeon in the Congo in its colonial days. Charles's father, Walter Fisher, had also been a medico, one of the first doctors who went to work with my grandfather in his mission in the Congo.

One year, our family was visiting Greystones, the lovely granite house that Charles Fisher had built on the banks of the Kafue River. In the evening, my parents were enjoying a sundowner with Charles and his wife Monica on the verandah overlooking the river.

'What do you want to do when you grow up, Richard?' Charles Fisher suddenly asked me.

'I want to study medicine,' I replied. 'I want to be a surgeon.'

'I can't think of a finer career in medicine than being a surgeon,' Charles Fisher told me.

Neither could I. What attracted me about surgery was the immediacy of it, the fact that you could take sick patients, treat them and within a few days they would be better and out of hospital. I was too impatient, I suppose, to treat chronically ill patients or to oversee people in hospital for months with all sorts of diseases. That just wasn't my scene. I preferred to get somebody who was unwell, who had a problem, treat it, get the patient better and then move on to something else.

A family friend recommended the medical school of St Andrews University, on the east coast of Scotland, near Edinburgh. Peterhouse prepared its students for the joint Oxford/Cambridge entrance examination, which was accepted by every English and Scottish university. I passed and my mother and father decided to take my two brothers as well as myself back to the UK.

So, in 1959, only months before Harold Macmillan's 'winds of change' speech signalled the end of the British Empire, we took another peaceful saunter, this time on the *Braemar Castle*, past the British possessions along the East African coast; Zanzibar at Dar es Salaam, then Aden, up the Red Sea, to Egypt, which was already fully independent. Small Egyptian boys demonstrated their affection by exposing themselves as we sailed through the Suez Canal.

Life at St Andrews University was every bit as good as I anticipated. My mother and father came to see me settled in St Salvators, a college there which had been founded in 1450. The university combined tradition with eruditeness, and (often bad) undergraduate medical jokes. The medical students' initiation ceremony was known as *bejant* heckling; the first-year person had to stand on a table and put up with being cross-examined and quizzed for a few minutes. 'How many spokes are there in a menstrual cycle?' was one question. The president of the student medical society controlled proceedings using a human femur bone as a gavel. I suppose the noise and clamour amounted to a very mild hazing. Over my time at St Andrews, I encountered many very senior medical men, and I remember thinking one night as some of these kilted, dinner-jacketed old gentlemen climbed on to tables and sang ribald songs, that maybe I would fit into the medical profession very comfortably.

During that very first term, my entire medical career nearly came to an end. One Saturday afternoon, a fellow student and I climbed the tower of the town's ruined medieval cathedral. He was also an experienced rock climber, and planned to leave medical school anyway. When we had nearly reached the top of the tower, a crowd gathered, the police arrived and we were ordered down.

The two of us were taken to the police station and charged with defacing an ancient monument. (Not half as much, I might say, as the defacement caused by the local hero John Knox, who stirred up the mob that wrecked the cathedral in the 1550s.)

Next, we were paraded, so to speak, before the master of St Salvators. Decked out in full academic rig, he formally announced that we were to be expelled on the spot. However, as my co-accused was distantly related to him, and planning to leave anyway, the master commuted our sentences to being gated for the remainder of the term.

At St Andrews, too, began my life-long study of flying. The

University Air Squadron (part of the Royal Air Force) provided uniforms, weekend accommodation, and taught anyone who was interested to fly. We trained in De Havilland Chipmunks at various RAF bases around the east coast.

Just as with my medical career, my flying career almost came to a gruesome early finish. This time, though, I did something right. Making only my second solo flight at RAF, Manby, in Lincolnshire, before takeoff I had to wait at a holding point to allow a flight of giant RAF Vulcan nuclear bombers to clear the runway. I was stuck at the hold point with my engine idling for more than fifteen minutes. As soon as I got into the air, my plane began to vibrate alarmingly. I thought an engine mounting had shaken loose, and that the engine was about to fall off the plane, and to the ground; to be followed shortly by the rest of the plane and me.

The one bit of training that kept running through my head was, 'Whatever happens, fly the aircraft.' I forgot correct procedure though, and pressed the transmit button and just called, 'Help.'

The tower responded, fairly laconically I thought, and I explained my problem. I still had partial power. I throttled back, made a gentle turn downwind at low level, and was able to land safely back on the Manby runway. My instructor ran up and wanted to know what the f— I thought I was up to. Fortunately, the engine repeated its vibrating after a couple of tries. The trouble turned out to be a stripped magneto which may have been caused by the prolonged idling. So instead of being pasted all over the green fields of Lincolnshire, I was officially commended in RAF flight news for 'cool-headed reaction to a potentially dangerous situation'.

At the end of my first year of medical studies, I failed my chemistry examination. To prepare for the re-sit, I went to the island of Rhum in the Western Hebrides, where I expected to be able to study peacefully. Commander Bill Harrison, a near neighbour there, and a Royal Navy veteran, ran a tourist boat around the islands, and introduced me to naval gin: half a glass of straight gin with some bitters; 'Too strong is it eh, lad? Have some more bitters in it.' Later,

Bill took me to visit one of the Royal Navy frigates then based at Rosyth Dockyard near Edinburgh, and engaged in protection of British fisheries. The naval hospitality was so overwhelming that Bill became too legless even to row a small boat in a placid harbour. I had to find my own way home in the dark.

Nevertheless, the upshot of my study vacation in the Western Hebrides was that I passed the re-sit chemistry exam. And I made sure it was the last exam I failed.

Over the following two years, study became more serious, as we began anatomy and physiology. I made a laughing stock of myself once by suggesting to our anatomy professor that the prostate gland is the size of an apple. Amid roars of laughter, he informed me that it is more the size of a walnut. The class year book for 1965 captioned my own portrait, 'Can you guess the size of Arnot's prostate?'

I spent one long vacation chasing a fellow student from St Andrews called Sue across the USA, and worked for a while at Toronto General Hospital as a porter, which enabled me to see a number of interesting operations.

Next long vacation, I went to Spain, again with Sue. We hitch-hiked around Spain, ran with the bulls at Pamplona, read Hemingway, and looked down on other tourists.

Before I left St Andrews, a friend and I tried climbing up the outside of one of the university buildings, this time without getting into trouble.

Lord Boothby (formerly Sir Robert, and one of Churchill's inner circle during the 1930s and 1940s) was installed as rector of the university while I was there. The great man lived up to his reputation and the rectorial procession through the small town of St Andrews became something of a pub crawl. Later I found there was yet another side to Sir Robert; he had been the lover of Lady Dorothy Macmillan (Prime Minister Sir Harold's wife) for about twenty years.

Following three marvellous years at St Andrews, we had to transfer across the River Tay to Queen's College to attend the teaching hospital and begin clinical training. Up until then, our only contact with humans had been in the form of corpses.

I worked harder than ever at Queen's, and in June 1965 I graduated Bachelor of Medicine, Bachelor of Surgery. I was lucky enough to get my first house job as what would generally be called an intern in the Professorial Department of Surgery at the Dundee Royal Infirmary. I was to spend the first six months of my training there.

Like all medical interns, I was worked exceptionally hard, over 120 hours a week. Often I was so tired, I slept in my clothes. I still do not quite understand what purpose this treatment serves. Several times fatigue caused me to make stupid mistakes. Once, to change the dressings on a twelve-year-old burns victim, I gave him pethidine intravenously, to relieve the pain of the procedure. Overtired, I inadvertently gave the lad an adult-sized dose. I had to walk him up and down the ward for fifteen minutes to keep him awake until the effects of the overdose wore off.

As luck would have it though, on my first Christmas at Dundee Royal Infirmary, my strong head for liquor won me my first try at surgery. The registrar who was on that night became quite tiddly after a few celebratory beers. Confronted with an acutely inflamed appendix that had to be cut out straight away, he handed me the scalpel, and went and sat in the corner of the operating room. He continued to sit quietly as I dealt with another two appendixes through the night.

The second six months of my medical training were spent at the other end of the country at the West Cornwall Hospital in Penzance. It has remained in my memory as my ideal sized hospital: big enough to have adequate equipment, and small enough to retain the personal touch that in critical cases can make the difference between life and death.

My father's characteristic gregariousness brought about my next career move. He loved to chat to people whom he encountered around the world, and one afternoon in Norway got talking with a fellow passenger on a holiday cruise. His new friend turned out to be a director of P&O, who helped me obtain an interview with that line's personnel department. So, on 12 September 1966, I sailed from Southampton on the 45 000 ton liner SS *Canberra* as deputy ship's surgeon. We were at the beginning of a three-month voyage around the world, via the Canary Islands, the Caribbean, the Panama Canal, New Zealand, Australia, Hong Kong and Japan.

When I set sail, I fully intended to devote my time at sea to studying for my primary FRCS (Fellowship of the Royal College of Surgeons) examination. I had subscribed to the correspondence course offered by the College. However, I soon found the social life on board ship to be too distracting to allow serious study. I decided to postpone the work until I had finished my voyaging.

Passengers on the *Canberra* for that cruise were an extraordinary mixture of ten quid migrants destined for Australia, and the rich and famous – including Cary Grant and his wife Dyan Cannon. I managed to embarrass myself by congratulating Cary Grant on his role in *To Kill a Mocking Bird*. Luckily, I was only talking to Dyan Cannon at the time. Cary Grant was out of earshot. After she finished laughing and pointing out the difference between her husband and Gregory Peck, she kindly promised not to tell Cary Grant about my faux pas. Whether she told him or not, he continued to greet me warmly in the saloon every morning with a great loud, 'Hi Doc', and a big wave of the hand.

Officers of the P&O company were looked after royally, and expected always to dress the part. To make quite certain of this, the company provided us with a servant, that is, a batman or steward. There were hundreds of stewards on *Canberra*, and their quarters were very picturesque. As deputy ship's doctor, I was obliged to inspect crew accommodation frequently. The pin-ups and decorations, and the bunks with pink lace curtains made the stewards' cabins look like a Soho brothel.

Following days of sun and quiet blue seas, we passed through the Panama Canal. We travelled up the west coast to Los Angeles where Cary Grant and Dyan Cannon left us. There was a stop in San

Francisco, and then another in Vancouver. Shortly, we turned out into the Pacific and sailed gently to Hawaii, where we stopped for a couple more days.

From there, *Canberra* sailed quietly and serenely across thousands of kilometres of mirror smooth, blue South Pacific Ocean to New Zealand. We stopped in Auckland briefly, before we set off for Sydney.

In one's life there are moments etched so sharp that they can never be lost. For me, our dawn arrival at the mouth of Sydney Harbour is one of those. The early morning mist cleared and revealed first, North Head, and South Head; between them the expanse of the harbour that Captain Phillip sailed over at the very beginning of history of the nation of Australia. We passed slowly down the great harbour to Circular Quay.

We had barely three days' shore leave in Sydney. One night, sitting in the dark on Bondi Beach, listening to the breakers rolling up on to the sand, I swore I would come back to Australia.

After a three-week side-cruise around Japan and Hong Kong, we took on passengers of another breed from Sydney, young Australians making for London; and English migrants returning to Britain, the latter known as returned empties. We travelled via Melbourne and Fremantle, to Colombo, then through the Suez Canal, to Lisbon and home.

Much as I enjoyed the voyaging, and the shipboard social life, I had become discontented. The senior surgeon on the *Canberra* had been collecting most of the fees, despite fobbing off a lot of the after hours work on to me. I decided to change ships as soon as I could. The Union Castle Shipping Company offered me a post on the *Cape Town Castle*, a veteran ocean liner, which was heading off for South Africa. It turned out to be the ship on which my parents had met each other in 1938, during its maiden voyage. The contrast with the *Canberra*, one of the biggest passenger ships afloat, and my new ship was marked. Nevertheless, I thoroughly enjoyed working on my new ship, and my new master, Captain Douglas Sowden.

As ship's surgeon, I was now one of the senior officers. Every morning we were obliged to meet for ship's rounds. The conference was usually preceded by Doug pouring himself a large pink gin, which he justified as, 'Just to steady me down, doctor.' Ship's rounds invariably concluded in one of the passenger lounges with a couple of stiffeners before lunch.

Doug enjoyed having a doctor at hand, whom after years at sea with no medical help at hand, he regarded as his personal physician. I grew to like Doug enormously. On a couple of voyages, he brought his 'treasure', his wife with him. He loved introducing her around the ship.

Early on in that first voyage, one of the *Cape Town Castle* cabin boys consulted me with appendicitis. I judged it would settle with conservative care, in other words, no surgical treatment. However it did not settle at all, and I had to operate on him the following day. Captain Doug brought the ship around into the wind and slowed her down to reduce the pitching and rolling as much as possible. The surgery was particularly difficult, because I had to supervise the general anaesthetic and operate at the same time. The hospital attendant I needed to hold the anaesthetic mask was fairly defective in the brain department and had to be watched very carefully. Doug strolled in several times during the operation with offers of help. The patient remained unwell after the operation, but came good after we stopped at Dakar, capital of Senegal in West Africa, for additional supplies of intravenous tetracycline.

Captain Doug was a veteran of the war in the Atlantic, during which he had managed to sink a U-boat from the armed merchant vessel he was commanding. Ever afterwards, Doug loved a bit of dramatic relief from the mundane life of cruising. So when we were radioed for help by a tramp steamer with another case of suspected appendicitis aboard, Doug straight away turned the ship around, and sailed off to help. The tramp steamer lowered one of her decrepit-looking lifeboats to ferry me over for a visit. The boat engine was kept cool by throwing a bucket of seawater over it every now and then.

Arriving beside the cargo ship, I clambered up a rope ladder dropped over the side, and found one of the junior officers did indeed have acute appendicitis. He was transferred onto a Stryker frame, trussed like a chicken, and lowered over the side into the lifeboat. When the patient was aboard, the boatswain of the lifeboat made to step from the rope ladder on to the heaving small boat. He slipped and fell, and planted his knee directly on the swollen abdomen of the patient, who fainted from the pain.

Back eventually, aboard the *Cape Town Castle*, we prepared the patient for surgery. Remembering the trouble I had had with the anaesthesia during the previous operation, this time, I used heavy sedation and local anaesthetic. I removed a gangrenous perforated appendix.

Only two days later, the young man was up and about. He was well enough, and he was determined not to waste his opportunities. He had been at sea for three months when we picked him up, and now he seemed more than pleased to be able to associate with the passengers.

Later, when he wrote to thank me for the operation, he informed me that he had not wasted his time on recuperation but instead, had slept with four of the passengers.

Life aboard the *Cape Town Castle* was very gregarious, and as with all ocean liners, the officers were expected to entertain the passengers. We were allotted a generous grog ration to help with our social duties. One evening Captain Doug criticised the black velvet (Guinness and champagne) I was serving my guests, and insisted that the already fairly deadly concoction needed reinforcement with the addition of a bottle or so of rum. The other guests seemed to like that well enough, and my party was a great success.

Following a year of mental atrophy and liver abuse on the *Canberra* and the *Cape Town Castle*, and after a brief holiday in Spain and Morocco, I went to work in South Africa. I began demonstrating anatomy at the University of Cape Town, that is, working as a junior lecturer. Trevor Jones, who had mended my broken ankle after a rock-climbing fall during my school days in Rhodesia, was now running the anatomy department and when we met during a break in my voyaging, he offered me the job while I began my long postponed preparation for FRCS exams.

The time at sea had been a useful break from years of university work, and now I was able to study harder than ever. Twelve months later, I sat the FRCS primary examination, and later that year I travelled to England for my brother's wedding. I met up with a good friend and colleague, John Kruger, and together we travelled to Athens. After illegally scaling the Acropolis by the light of the moon and visiting the Minoan palace of Knossos on Crete, we returned to Cape Town to resume our surgical life.

Having passed the primary examination, we joined the casualty department at Groote Schuur hospital to increase our experience of trauma surgery. Because of the way South African life was in those days, the department was unbelievably busy. During one twelve-hour shift that sticks in my mind, John Kruger and I treated 157 patients, many of them seriously injured from gunshot wounds or motor vehicle accidents. As well, I inserted hundreds of sutures into multiple stab wounds.

On another, less fraught evening, I turned to the med student hovering at my shoulder and asked him to take care of a Xhosa woman who had recently been brought in and was in the throes of giving birth. I walked off to look at other patients.

Soon, the student returned, now looking very worried and pale. 'Doc, you are not going to believe this but the little bugger has crawled back inside.' He told me that he had delivered the baby, turned his back for a moment, then looked at his patient to find the baby's legs disappearing back inside his mother again. I was puzzled myself. I rushed to the cubicle, and yes, there were a pair of legs where he said. Then, I pulled the blankets back to show the first twin lying quietly sucking his thumb, waiting to be joined by his brother who was only half way there. This was what is known as a breech birth as babies are normally born head-first. This sort of delivery is more dangerous than the normal head-first arrival, but in this case the baby was small and was delivered without complication.

In 1972, I sat the exam in Edinburgh for the final FRCS examination, and passed on my first attempt. The exam included a viva voce section, that is, answering questions on any aspect of surgery put by a panel of surgeons. Obviously, each result is known more or less straight away. Having finished the exam, we nervous candidates stood around in the college foyer while the names of the successful surgeons were read out. Later, as we shared a sherry with the Fellows, I began for the first time in my life to feel like a real surgeon.

My professor of surgery at Cape Town was very helpful, despite, I suspect, his disapproval of my character and talents. He suggested that I begin work in the surgical research department where Christiaan Barnard had recently conducted on baboons the heart transplant studies that were to write the names of Groote Schuur hospital and Christiaan Barnard into medical history.

My own task was to undertake a research project to study why experimental pigs used for liver transplant research developed fatal gastric ulcers. Thus, serendipitously, I became involved in gastroenterology. It has remained my major surgical interest ever since. I spent two years studying the gastric physiology of pigs, using small pouches of stomach which secreted acid and pepsin in response to injections of certain drugs. I wrote a thesis entitled 'Hepatic and biliary factors in oesophago-gastric ulceration in pigs'. I was awarded the Master of Surgery by the University of Cape Town. During this time I met and married Penelope Thornton, from Yorkshire.

Penny and I decided in 1974, that we did not want to bring up our two children, William and Lucy, in an increasingly violent, and repressive, South Africa.

We moved back to the UK, and I began work in Scarborough as surgical registrar under an outstanding surgeon, Alan Pollock. Of all the surgical jobs I had in Britain those twelve months at Scarborough with Alan, a dynamic surgeon and researcher if ever there was one, turned out to be the most useful. At Scarborough, I consolidated my interest in clinical surgical research.

After the busy year in Scarborough, I was appointed to a temporary post in Bristol Royal Infirmary as lecturer/senior registrar in surgery. That should have been the making of my career, but my marriage was beginning to break down and, unfortunately, that strain affected my work. After a fairly unsuccessful year in Bristol, I began work as a surgical oncologist at the Royal Marsden Hospital in London.

Money remained tight, and Penny was still unhappy. An existence of toing and froing by motor bike on cold winter mornings from our house in South London, began to pall on me, too. We searched for opportunities. Soon, we had the bright idea of a life in the sun in Jeddah, Saudi Arabia.

I just hadn't foreseen that we would be in the sun, but in gaol to boot.

A very dangerous liaison

My dreams of sunshine, and well-rewarded hard work had crumbled into a sordid existence in Jeddah's Ruwais prison. Penny meanwhile had confessed her way into a possible death sentence.

Shortly after Tim Hayter admitted their behaviour to me, I had an equally disturbing conversation with Penny. She had been brought down to see me from the women's prison. I hadn't seen her for days.

'I'm sorry at having caused you so much trouble, Richard,' Penny began, alluding to her liaison with Tim.

'What a bloody silly thing to do,' was my first response. 'Why did you tell them?' I asked.

She looked at me in silence.

'I'm worried,' I told her. 'We haven't been charged with anything. What do you suppose that means? I can't understand why we are being held like this.'

She shook her head in despair.

We were sitting opposite one another, in the prison governor's office, with several guards in attendance. Captain Saad, the second in command, the deputy governor of Ruwais prison, sat nearby. It was Monday 11 June; day 23 of our incarceration.

Having sex with Tim was one thing but admitting it to the police was quite another. Did she realise then, had either of us grasped, that she had unwittingly admitted to a capital offence?

'I couldn't help it, Richard,' she sobbed, 'I had no choice, I was feeling terrible.'

'I know, I know. We are all feeling terrible. But why didn't you tell me about Tim?'

She cast her eyes down.

'I'm sorry at having caused you so much trouble, Richard,' she repeated.

'Well, it's done now,' I replied philosophically, 'Tim told me anyway.'

She looked at me with sad eyes.

'Regret is a useless emotion,' I added.

'Oh, but I don't regret anything,' she parried. 'I'm just sorry it has come to this.'

'What?' I could not believe what she was saying. Here I was, feeling magnanimous, prepared to forgive her.

'Penny, how can you say that?' I tried to explain how I felt but it was difficult with such a crowd around.

'I think we should leave this until we have some more privacy,' I conceded and Penny nodded in agreement.

In prison, I saw Penny from time to time. Our meetings were usually tense and strained, but that is the one that sticks in my memory.

Back in my cell, I stewed over the conversation.

There was no great anger in me about Penny's liaison with Tim. There was just sadness and disappointment. It was more my feeling of betrayal. And that was nothing new.

Penny had always been a flirt. During our eight years of marriage, I had turned a blind eye to a few indiscretions. Yet Penny herself was very jealous, often questioning my behaviour – and there certainly was no cause for that. She was disturbed by the tiniest incidents. Even during my time in Ruwais prison, Penny became jealous of Sue McCormack from the Australian Embassy, who visited me in prison and sent me books.

◻◩◻

I first met Penny at a drinks party in Cape Town in November 1968. Among the thirty or so guests, I straight away noticed a tall, attractive woman with dark, shoulder length hair. Dressed in a striking white blouse and slacks, in contrast to the other women who wore dresses, I was attracted to her gregarious personality and her broad smile.

'Richard Arnot. How do you do?'

'Penelope Thornton. Pleased to meet you.'

She was very attractive, vivacious and had quite a broad sense of humour which I liked. Penny was outgoing, loved male company and, what was to be our downfall, was a terrific flirt.

'May I give you a lift?' I offered, on discovering she had no transport back to her accommodation.

'That would be lovely.'

She was impressed by my dark blue MG sports car and I felt rather smart and smooth, more so when I opened the glove compartment and took out a scarf. I had always kept one there, just in case.

'You may like to use this so your hair doesn't blow in the wind,' I said, feeling rather suave and debonair.

She took it gratefully from my hand and, when she agreed to see me again, I was delighted.

Her father had been a lieutenant colonel in the British Royal Artillery and her mother a member of the Women's Royal Army Corps (the WRACs). Penny was born in Germany, while her father was stationed there after World War II as part of the British occupation forces.

Penny contracted polio at the age of two and this had left her with a thin weakened right leg and a limp. So she preferred to wear trousers. Because of her leg, we couldn't do much walking and climbing, the sorts of things that I really enjoyed, but we used to go camping in the hills with friends. We also went to the beach quite often.

I found I was becoming romantically attracted to Penny. So I felt somewhat dismayed when she told me one day, 'John is coming from England to visit me next week. He's my fiancé.'

'Fiancé? You didn't tell me you had a fiancé.'

She smiled. 'Yes, but it's all over.'

Apparently John had come to try and resuscitate things. Fortunately for me, that didn't work out.

Penny and I saw increasing amounts of one another and, as time went on, I fell very much in love with her, so much so that I was prepared to accept a certain amount of flirting – that was just part of her nature.

Not long after meeting Penny, I got my primary surgical fellowship and entered the surgery department. The work was very hard and the relationship with Penny became strained. She liked a lot of attention and there was conflict from the start. But it was just one of those things. I hoped I could resolve it.

Eventually, Penny and I were married in Wakefield Cathedral, Yorkshire on 25 July 1970. Our son, William, was born the following year and our daughter, Lucy, in 1973.

We argued a lot. We were always arguing about money. We never had enough of that. Penny liked the good life, she liked to do things in style and there was constant friction. Finances were tough. What with a large mortgage, and our two young children to feed, clothe and educate, my income was often stretched paying for the costly furniture and clothes the lifestyle demanded.

Then came the bright idea I have already mentioned; move to the sun, make more money. It came to us one evening, over a gin and tonic. Penny suddenly turned to me and said, 'Why don't we leave all this and go and make some real money?'

It was a good thought. Many doctors were emigrating. One of my colleagues had just gone to America and another to the Channel Islands. Disillusionment with the National Health Service was growing. We were all expected to do more and more, examining and treating an ever increasing number of patients with fewer staff, no clerical back-up and minimal salary increases. At my previous surgical job, Bristol Royal Infirmary, the main surgical ward had not been upgraded for over thirty years. The floor was covered with worn and pitted linoleum. The ward was twenty years behind the times even then, with the forty beds lined up, only seventy-five centimetres apart, along the room in an outdated Florence Nightingale style. And just down the road stood the brand new, fully carpeted and furnished tower block where the administrators were housed.

'Where do you suggest?'

'Somewhere warm.'

That single specification was immediately attractive. Winter was fast approaching. Our social life tended to be fairly quiet. With my long working hours and our two young children, we could manage only the occasional party and missed out on the cultural opportunities that London had to offer. The weekends I did have free we spent driving out along the M4 motorway to visit my mother, who lived in the Cotswold village of Sheepscombe, or to Penny's mother in Dorset.

'Somewhere warm,' I echoed.

'Yes. Why not the Middle East?'

Penny fetched an atlas and we looked through it.

'How about Dubai?'

'Yes or Abu Dhabi. Do you know anyone who has worked there?'

'Mmm, I don't think so. How about Qatar?'

'Possibly.'

One thing, however, we were both agreed on. We were prepared to travel and work anywhere in the Middle East. Anywhere. Except for Saudi Arabia. I had been there a year earlier, on a five-week locum job. Although it had been fun for a while, I did not relish being in Saudi Arabia with a wife and family. Taking them into a country where women are forbidden to drive cars or go out alone, where alcohol is banned, where life for Westerners is restricted in so many ways, could make for a difficult and arduous time. Why would I deliberately seek that out?

That night I found it difficult to sleep, pondering on our future. A mixture of excitement tinged with apprehension kept me tossing and turning until the early hours of the morning. Next day I rang several medical employment agents. The first job I was offered was, of all places, located in Jeddah, in Saudi Arabia.

'We are interviewing this afternoon. Can you attend?'

Why was I even considering this position, I asked myself? Penny and I had decided against Saudi Arabia. Why didn't I decline immediately? Why did I look further at the details of this position? Curiosity, I decided. Studying this job would give me a starting point, show me what is on offer overseas, I told myself.

'An interview this afternoon? Ah, not this afternoon,' I replied.

'Tomorrow?'

'I am not available tomorrow. May I get back to you?'

Hurriedly looking through my appointment book, I saw some free time two days hence.

That afternoon, I took a taxi to Piccadilly to meet my prospective employer. I entered a building off a side street and climbed the stairs to a small office. Dr Abdul Rahman Taha Bakhsh rose from his chair to greet me.

Dr Bakhsh had thickset features and a pleasant reassuring smile. He wore a white *thobe* and head dress. He did not look Arab and I only discovered later that he was of Pakistani extraction. His English was halting but we were able to communicate fluently. Dr Bakhsh was the owner of a new hospital which was in its final construction stages. The interview was pleasantly informal. After ninety minutes, I was offered the job. My resolve weakened with every inducement.

The position in Jeddah sounded very attractive; a brand new hospital, fully equipped and staffed entirely by British doctors and nurses, a salary almost double my National Health Service pay, with the added bonus that the money was tax free. Such a financial status would be ideal for our blossoming overdraft. But what attracted me most was the job itself.

The successful applicant would be head of a brand new surgical unit with the latest fibre-optic, endoscopic and gastroscopic facilities. He would oversee a staff of British-trained Arab surgeons and British-trained theatre nurses.

'Never before has there been such a hospital with such staff and such equipment in Jeddah. I want to offer patients the best possible surgical care in Jeddah. You will be provided with free accommodation, a fully furnished, air-conditioned flat in the centre of town. Naturally the children will have free schooling. There is an excellent local school for expatriate children.'

This was getting better and better. My earlier qualms were fading. I would take the job if he offered it.

He did.

'And you accept?'

'I have to give it some thought and discuss this with my wife. I will ring you with my decision.'

He gave me five days.

Penny was hesitant. I could not understand her.

'Do you really want to stay on in the UK, like this?' I began. 'The weather's lousy. I'm always overworked. The money's not brilliant. Just think – two years in Saudi Arabia and we can come back with enough cash to set us up properly.'

Penny was a lot more cautious and sceptical than I was. I am by nature trusting, perhaps too much so, and I believed all that I had been told about the job.

Still, Penny did not entirely dismiss the offer. Intrigued by my enthusiasm, she accompanied me to Dr Bakhsh's office.

'I don't trust him,' she informed me afterwards.

'Why not?'

'He has shifty eyes.'

I laughed. 'Don't be silly. Surely you agree the job sounds terrific?'

'Yes, I suppose so. But what about me and the children? I don't fancy being confined to the house. You know just how restricted life is for Western women in Saudi Arabia. It's far worse than in other Middle Eastern countries.'

We did have to consider the children. How would the move affect them? Seven-year-old William and five-year-old Lucy were as different in appearance as in personality. A quiet introspective child, our son had a calm but confident demeanour. His cheeky grin contrasted with the angelic look of his blond hair, a thick mane that stood out from his head like a halo if not cut frequently. Lucy, on the other hand, was a noisy, outgoing child. Both of them were highly excited at the prospect of a move to Jeddah. But that was my doing. For their knowledge of the Middle East had been gleaned from me.

Although I had spent a short time there, I still had a glamorised view of the Middle East, based on exotic Hollywood movies; images of vast sand-duned landscapes and white-robed riders, palm trees and oases providing respite from the scorching sun. As a youngster I had read *The Seven Pillars of Wisdom* and had been captivated by the images of its author, British Army officer T. E. Lawrence, sitting on his camel, resplendent in full Arab regalia. I had been entranced by the colourful accounts of his desert exploits.

Penny kept on, 'Oh, Richard. I keep telling you, it's all too easy. It sounds too good to be true.'

I kept pushing the issue with her. For I also had another reason for accepting the job. We had now been married for eight years, and our relationship was not the best. It was frequently tense and strained. Perhaps a new foundation in another country would give us a fresh start.

Finally, Penny reluctantly acceded to my wishes.

On a Saturday morning, at nine o'clock, I rang Dr Bakhsh.

'I accept.'

◻◲◻

From our first moments in Jeddah, Penny was not happy. With some reason, I believe. That discontent was over comparatively trivial issues however: dust, heat, freedom to go to the shops, to drive a car. Now, in prison, waiting to be charged, Penny faced savage retribution for conduct many in the West would have considered a mere peccadillo.

In a country ruled by sharia law, adultery must either be confessed to or witnessed by four people (in practice, four adult males). Otherwise the accused can just say, 'No, it never happened', and that is the end of the matter.

Penny, however, had admitted adultery. Tim, on being challenged with her information, had confirmed it. Neither of them realised the severe implications at the time and the fatal consequences.

Adultery carries the penalty of death by stoning in Saudi Arabia. That Penny could be facing a death penalty was not explained to us for quite some time. There was an enormous cry of outrage in the British newspapers, but none of us on the spot really knew what was going on.

On Penny's next visit, she gasped, 'What a relief to see you, Richard.' She looked shaken. I revived her with a Pepsi, and some multivitamin tablets as well as medication for the gut colic she had developed.

'I am so worried,' she told me, on the verge of tears, 'what will they do to me? It's just so awful waiting and waiting with no word. I'm so scared that they'll –'

She faltered.

'There's no way they'll give you the death penalty. Dr Bakhsh said so,' I told her firmly. 'They won't apply Islamic law to you.'

'Won't they, Richard? How do you know that? How does anyone know that? You're just trying to calm me down.'

And I was. But they couldn't, surely they wouldn't, apply Islamic law to a Western woman?

Or would they?

'Richard,' she began hesitantly, 'you know I've had to stop taking the tablets –'

'Yes.'

'Well, well – I'm frightened of having a relapse when I get out.'

Penny had been depressed for quite a long time and had been on medication for periods during our marriage in England and now here, in Saudi Arabia. I suppose it could have been reactive depression to our poor relationship and the stresses of life in

Jeddah. Yet whatever the reason, the antidepressant tablets altered the chemical balance in her brain and restored her to a much happier frame of mind.

Now, however, because of the strict prison policy which forbade drugs of any type, she had had abruptly to stop the course of treatment. Such a sudden cessation, rather than cutting down gradually, was inadvisable from a physiological point of view. She had good reason to fear a setback.

I understood her qualms.

But I tried to reassure her.

'Penny, I think you are doing splendidly under the circumstances. You're off the pills and you're coping by yourself in another section of the prison. I'm with the others, after all, but you're all alone, with no support.'

'Mmm, I suppose so.'

'Really, darling, I'm most impressed at how well you are doing.'

I truly admired the way Penny was coping. Aside from the harsh conditions, violence was not unknown in the women's block. Quite recently a big fight had broken out, and a female officer was attacked for not having reported a broken drinking water machine.

As well as her general isolation, Penny had to cope with other stresses, such as her only friend's suicide attempt. 'She slashed her wrists with the blade from a pencil sharpener,' Penny told me. 'Everyone just stood around and watched while I bandaged her up and cleaned up the mess. It was awful, truly awful. The guards refused to carry her to the clinic. They just dragged her.'

I still pushed hard for Penny to be released. If there was to be any problem over the party, any punishment, then I would deal with that. I constantly campaigned for her release – with Captain Saad, with Francis Geere from the embassy, with anyone and everyone who would listen to me.

Set Penny free.

But she had inadvertently spoken of her own crime. A crime for which she would have to be punished.

Men in prison

The prisoners in my cell were a varied lot. Old Ali was the cell boss. A man in his fifties with a small goatee beard, he sometimes led the prayers. He was in for embezzlement.

Ahmed, who came from Mecca, was accused of molesting a girl. His great ambition on release was to visit a brothel in Damascus of which he had heard. There he would sip Johnnie Walker Red Label whisky from a whore's navel.

Abdul was serving a four-year sentence for drugs. He had been caught with four grams of pot.

Young Ali was a pleasant lad aged about twenty. He was awaiting execution. His crime was that he had killed a man who had raped him. Ali's mistake was he then tried to get rid of the body by burning it. He then made off in the man's car. The victim's family wanted his head, but Ali's family were trying to buy them off.

Each Thursday young Ali fell silent and refused to eat. Executions took place on Fridays, but no warning was given to those awaiting death. The prisoner would only know of it when the guards came early on Friday morning to chain him up and escort him on the one-way trip to the market place. Public beheadings took place there after noon prayers.

Thankfully I never witnessed an execution during my time in Saudi Arabia but someone I knew at the Australian Embassy did, inadvertently caught up in the crowd at the wrong time. He described to me how the hapless prisoner's head was literally hacked off, the inexperienced soldier taking several swipes with his sword to sever the neck while the dying man struggled and writhed in the dust.

A Pakistani fellow prisoner had to endure two years in prison for possessing a 'sexy pen'.

'A sexy pen?' I inquired.

'Yes. There is a female figure inside it and, when you turn the pen upside down, her swimsuit comes off and she is naked,' he told me.

Two years of his life forfeited for a silly pen.

But at least he was left alone to serve his time. Others were less fortunate. One foreigner I came across had been tortured. He claimed he had merely been carrying money, not alcohol. Nevertheless, the police assumed the cash had come from supplying liquor. He had been whipped, handcuffed to a bed for twelve hours, burnt with cigarettes. He had been given electric shocks and the fingernails on one hand had been pulled out. He had had no contact with either his family or his embassy and, most amazing of all, no charges had been laid. I shuddered as he told me his story and cringed as he stretched out his hand before me.

An Italian, who had been caught smuggling alcohol, had endured torture and eight and a half months in solitary confinement. An Englishman, arrested for receiving backhanders on two air-conditioning units, had been in prison for almost three months and his case had still not been heard.

◙◙◙

Early in my time in Ruwais, I woke one morning feeling dreadful. I was very tired. The lights had been full on all night. The floor was a mass of bodies.

'My name is Morris,' I heard a voice beside me say.

'And mine is Richard.'

'Where are you from?'

'England. And you?'

It turned out Morris was Palestinian. He spoke English very well and had a fascinating but chilling story to relate, one of many alarming accounts that I was to hear over the following months.

Morris had been an acquaintance of a certain well-connected Saudi. Unbeknown to Morris, or so he told me, this man bungled the robbery of a money changer's store in the *souk*. The thief bribed two assistants for the keys, with which he managed to open the outer door but not the second. Wisely, he abandoned the attempt.

Months later he tried again, repeating the crime almost exactly. This time, he shot dead the two assistants. Only four hours later, he was on a plane to Beirut, with a suitcase containing nine million riyals.

But he had made two mistakes. One was leaving a spare pistol magazine in his hotel room; the other was telling a friend about the crime. The criminal did not realise that the friend was an informant for the Saudi police.

Picked up by Interpol, he was brought back to Jeddah. His two Yemeni drivers were also arrested as was Morris who protested his innocence. 'I know nothing about the robbery,' he said.

Interrogated, imprisoned and tortured over a period of four and a half years, Morris was eventually so worn down that he finally admitted to knowledge of the robbery and signed a false statement.

Soon afterwards, on a Friday morning, the four men were taken to the holding cell for condemned prisoners outside the mosque in the market square. After midday prayers, the others were taken off and decapitated.

Morris was brought back to Ruwais to serve out a sentence of ten years' imprisonment. On top of that, Morris received twenty lashes a week for the entire ten-year stretch. But, from what I could gather, the lashes were not that bad – less painful than any school caning. When I met Morris, he still had four years to go. He seemed surprisingly unruffled by his ill fortune.

I continued writing my diary, keeping a brief record of daily events and jotting down the stories of my fellow prisoners. By the time I was released, I considered myself a world expert in the pitfalls facing European business people trading with Arabs. There were plenty of tales of chicanery but two that have stuck in my mind concerned an American and an Englishman.

The American, a prisoner for nearly two years, had been thrown into gaol immediately on his arrival from the United States. He had struck a deal with an affluent Saudi to purchase jointly a fleet of prime movers in America. The purchase was to be financed by mortgage bonds transferred from Saudi Arabia. When the bonds proved to be bogus, the American halted the transaction. After some months of fruitless negotiations, his Saudi partner invited him to Jeddah to resolve the difficulty face to face.

Naively, the American accepted this offer. As soon as he arrived, he was arrested, accused of embezzlement and imprisoned until he released the trucks.

The Englishman, Graham Piper, who was also in prison with me, had a similar problem, albeit with a more painful outcome. He was in the transport business too, as a haulage contractor. He had set up a transcontinental line trucking overland between Britain and Saudi Arabia.

In Jeddah, Graham bought a trailer from a Saudi national. A day or two later, while he was moving some goods from the port the former owner suddenly appeared.

'Hey, that's my trailer. That man is driving my trailer,' shouted the Saudi.

The port authorities believed the word of the Arab over the foreigner, and locked up Graham pending inquiries. He protested his innocence vehemently. 'I bought the trailer. I have got papers to prove it.'

It took over a year for Graham's case to come before the court, and finally a Saudi judge found in his favour. The court agreed that, yes, Graham had indeed purchased the trailer.

'But the papers have not been stamped,' he was told.

'Stamped?'

'The papers must be stamped by the British Embassy because you are a British subject.'

'I'm sorry. I'll do that straight away.'

'That is an offence, ignorance of the law.'

It was trivial enough, but the authorities needed to save face. They had locked him up for no reason. So, for the lack of the pre-requisite stamp, he received fifty lashes with the cane.

I was interested in all of the prisoners and determined to talk to as many of them as I could. I had begun to learn Arabic while working at the Bakhsh Hospital. I now pursued it diligently. There was no shortage of willing teachers; Fathi who gave me regular lessons, Ahmed who used to read with me. In a surprisingly short time, within weeks of the daily lessons, I astonished myself by becoming fluent in the basic or street version of spoken Arabic, which is a lot easier to acquire than the official written language. Now I was able to communicate, albeit on a somewhat basic level, with those around me. I could hold my own in fascinating conversations with other prisoners. The men were open about their background and the more I spoke with them, the more extraordinary stories I heard.

One afternoon at the shop area, the mini souk between cell blocks, I talked to a Nigerian. An elderly man, he had a charming look about him and seemed approachable. I greeted him and he responded. He spoke only Arabic.

'What are you here for?' I asked.

'Haboob,' he responded, using the term for tablets or drugs.

He came from his home on the annual Hajj, the pilgrimage that all Muslims are supposed to make at least once in their lifetime. Foolishly he brought with him a suitcase full of Librium tablets to finance his journey. Caught by Customs at Jeddah airport, he had been in gaol ever since.

'How long have you been here?'

'I do not know. Many many years. I was a young man.'

'When do you think you will get out?'

His black face broke into a gentle smile at my naivete.

'I will die in prison,' he said, seeming to quite accept the fact. His plight indeed seemed hopeless. Early on he had tried to contact the British Embassy, who handled such affairs, there being no Nigerian representation then in Saudi Arabia, but he had had no response. (He was very unclear about dates, but I suspect that there was no Nigerian representation in Saudi Arabia at the time of his arrest because Nigeria was then still a British colony: in other words he had been in our prison since before 1960.)

He had had no response from anyone and had never been visited by any diplomatic staff. He had made no plans for the future and seemed settled in his way, having made a life for himself in prison. He was bedded. He was clothed. He was fed. His needs were met.

'Do you have family?'

'Yes, I have children in Nigeria.'

He had never heard from them and did not know anything about their lives since he had left.

The horror stories continued. Samir, a pleasant twenty-one year old, had served eight months in prison for being alone in a car with a woman.

'We were just driving,' he told me.

'Not kissing or anything?'

'No,' he looked shocked, 'just driving.'

In another cell of our block, there was a Malaysian dealer in gold and jewellery. He sold gold worth 650 000 riyals to a Saudi client, for an initial deposit of 170 000 riyals. The Malaysian dealer put up at the Meridien, and ran up a bill of 30 000 riyals while waiting for his customer to pay him the balance. Only then would he transfer the gold.

In the meantime, his Saudi customer contacted the police, and claimed that the Malaysian was going to flit with his deposit and not hand over the gold.

The police arrested the gold dealer. By the time I met him, he had been in prison for eight months. He had had one court appearance, where he was asked to repay the deposit and call it quits. I knew I was only hearing one side of the story, but whatever the truth of the situation, I had it driven home to me, yet again, that in Saudi Arabia the wheels of justice turned very, very slowly.

Early in our months of prison, my relationship with the Germans, although friendly, was not particularly close. They tended to stick together and, naturally enough, talked to one another in their native tongue. Over time, I did, however, get to know some of them better and took quite a liking to them.

Klaus Ritter was a real hoot. He was extremely fat, and had a great sense of humour. The Arabs were fond of him, obesity being a sign of status in their culture. I remember once when they played at worshipping him, bending down to kiss his feet while Klaus roared with laughter.

Martin Fleischer had quite a different time of it. 'They won't let me sit on the beds,' he complained to me once.

'Why not?'

He blushed.

I discovered it was because he didn't use water at a fundamental stage of his personal toileting.

Arab toilet etiquette was strict. Their method of wiping the bottom was to use the bare left hand with water on it and then to wash both hands after that. Martin refused to do this and used toilet paper instead, as most of us did. But somebody had spotted Martin using toilet paper and decided this wasn't clean enough. They were convinced that his bottom wasn't properly cleaned and so they wouldn't let him sit on the beds. Rather odd, I thought, considering the state of the lavatories.

For Martin and I, the two constants were Mohammed Masri, who was Egyptian, and Mahomed Abdul Karim. Mohammed Masri was a great peacemaker. He spoke fluent English and smoothed over many a wrinkle caused by Martin's Teutonic way of impinging on Arab sensitivity.

Mohammed Masri was a history teacher in Cairo. He was engaged to be married. In Saudi Arabia, he worked on a visitor's visa to make enough money to buy a flat in Cairo. When the visitor's visa expired, he forged an extension stamp in his passport. It fooled several officials, but was eventually spotted. Mohammed is labelled a dangerous prisoner and is not allowed to visit the doctor.

Martin was quite intimidated by the other prisoners' stories. Mahomed Abdul Karim, a twenty-three year old, told Martin how he had been travelling in a car with a friend. Both of them were drunk. The friend had been taunting him. Finally Karim pulled out a gun and shot his friend in the head. Now the friend's family wanted Karim executed but his own family were trying to talk them out of it.

Mahomed Abdul Karim later made me a very nice little cup-board. He told me he was only pulling Martin's leg with his story of shooting his friend. When Martin had arrived in Ruwais, he told Karim he was there because two people had died. Karim thought Martin meant he had killed them. So, not to be outdone, Karim told Martin he was there himself because he had shot his best friend.

Karim's real problem was that he had had a car accident after drinking half a bottle of whisky. The police had found the half bottle in his car together with a pistol he had kept there.

Mahomed Abdul Karim became my firm friend. I felt sorry for him while I thought he was due for execution, and when I found out he was an asthmatic, as I was, I got him a new Ventolin inhaler from outside. If others' fate was any guide, he would be in Ruwais for at least six months before the police got round to charging him.

I heard the story one day of a Nigerian who was found to have a forged $100 bill at the airport. While he was being transported into town, the guard holding the forged note and his papers mockingly told him he would probably be executed. The Nigerian got such a fright he grabbed the note and ate it, thus destroying the evidence.

Graham Piper, the English haulage contractor pointed out to me an American who had been in Ruwais for only three days. Despite being arrested with a bottle of whisky in his car, the American was released today and deported. His boss flew in and threw his weight around. It just shows how quickly things can be done when someone puts his foot down and gets a move on. Also how well the Yanks are treated here in comparison with us, especially when they work for large companies with a major Saudi government interest.

◧◪◧

Jacques Texier is in another cell block, but I am able to talk to him occasionally. He told me of a man in his cell who killed someone in a fight. The victim's sons are thirteen and fourteen years old. But Jacques' section mate has to wait seven years until they come of age and are able to decide whether they want his head or his blood money...

A young Filipino admitted to our section a few days ago had been arrested in the souk while he was trying to buy a watch. He kept pointing at the one he wanted but couldn't get the Saudi stall-holder to understand. So the Filipino leant over the counter to point more closely. The Arab grabbed him by the shirt front, accused him of trying to steal the watch and yelled for the police...

The Filipino was taken to the Sharifia. He had been strung up in manacles and beaten for three days to make him confess. Then he was brought to Ruwais. The lad's father was due to go back to the Philippines as his visa and contract had expired. The son will be left on his own...

An Egyptian baker, Hassan, nine months earlier flew to Jeddah on Egyptair. A friend asked him to take a present over for someone. Inside was concealed half a kilogram of hash; found by Customs. He has not been to court yet...

Young Ali, the nice lad in our section, is still under sentence of death. Every Friday morning since I have been here he shits himself half to death, as the gendarmes might arrive unannounced, chain him up and take him down to the market square to have his head cut off...

Another of my fellow prisoners was a university student from Mecca. In the street one day, he recognised another student, a young

woman, sitting in a car and went to speak to her through the car
window. Suddenly her father appeared and had him arrested for
importuning his daughter. He had been in prison for six months by
the time he told me his story…

The 'Jeddah Axeman' was an Australian engineer who used to work for a construction company. He lived in barracks with other employees out in the desert. He had come to Saudi Arabia to escape from his alcoholism. But his problem continued to haunt him.

With no access to alcohol, the 'Axeman' became quite manic. During a dispute with another worker on the site, he picked up a hammer and struck him a mighty blow on the head. The victim made a partial recovery and was sent back to his native Britain a paraplegic with severe brain damage. The Australian was imprisoned. Release would only be possible after payment of blood money. With no money to his name and with no resources of any kind, the 'Axeman' seemed doomed to rot away his life in captivity. (Months later, I contacted the English victim after my return to Britain. He would not agree to releasing the 'Jeddah Axeman' until he had been paid. Some time later, however, I did hear that the Australian had been freed. So I guess the Saudi authorities may just have let him go.)

◧◩◨

Homosexuality in prison was amazing and quite overt, despite such activity being illegal in the Middle East. There were two types of pursuit: steady relationships, and the lads who prostituted themselves for money, watches or other valuables.

In my room, we had both. Whenever he has the chance, prisoner Abdullah makes straight for prisoner Yeh Yeh's bed and the two act like 'man and wife'. They cuddle together much of the day and are covered in love bites. I have never actually seen them have sex. In the other cell, though, another couple spend the entire time locked together, kissing one another, cuddling and caressing. How they manage to escape the gaze and inevitable wrath of the guards is extraordinary.

Then, in our room, one of the older prisoners, Gonfidi imported a sort of 'female' prostitute type, a floozy, an effeminate creature who pranced proudly about flaunting Gonfidi's watch (earned for services rendered). He represents a sex object to some of the Arabs. Meanwhile Old Ali, our cell leader, entices crowds of young lads into our cell.

Officially homosexuality is forbidden. Male to male intercourse is punishable by death in Saudi Arabia. But the guards only respond if their attention is drawn to it. Homosexual behaviour is rampant in prison and, as long as it is not reported or officially observed, it is accepted.

In Saudi Arabia, males and females are separated from the age of a few years, and boys only have occasional slight contact with female relatives until an arranged marriage takes place. Prior to that, I am told the lusty young lads use one another for sexual gratification.

Thankfully I was never approached in prison by any of the men for physical contact although I did experience one curious episode.

One of the inmates in my room was Aswad, the son of one-time Ethiopian slaves. (Slavery existed under cover in Saudi Arabia until as recently as 1962.) The word '*aswad*' means 'black' and Aswad, born in Saudi Arabia, was coal black.

One night, as I was undressing, I felt, uncomfortably, that I was being watched. Turning round, I found Aswad's eyes focused on my body. He addressed me in Arabic. 'How do you get that lovely white skin?' he asked. 'I really would like a white skin,' he mused.

I was flummoxed.

'What do you use?' he asked.

'Nothing. That's just the way I am.'

'What?' He appeared genuinely puzzled. 'I'm sure you can make skin like that, can't you?'

I thought he was joking at first but soon realised he was deadly serious.

'What bleach can I use?' he wanted to know.

'No,' I said gently, 'I'm white. He's slightly black,' I continued, pointing to one of the others in the room, 'and you're black. That's just the way we are.'

He did not understand. He felt sure that there was some way in which one could turn oneself white. And there I was trying to convince him that he couldn't do a Michael Jackson.

I developed a great deal of sympathy for my fellow prisoners during my time in gaol. I also came to realise just how futile a punishment prison really is, especially for hardened criminals. Regulars in Ruwais had made a comfortable life for themselves and prison held no fear for them.

I have often thought since that if I were threatened with imprisonment over, say, a matter of principle, I would have no hesitation in going back there again. And during those months in gaol, I conquered a subconscious fear that I think I had had all my life, something that might be described as a fear of fear itself. During those difficult months I lost that fear and it never came back.

◨◪◧

Prison diary

◨◪◧

FRIDAY 1 JUNE 1979

This business could linger on for a long time until they are satisfied they have exhausted every possibility.

The daily routine seems to be to stay in the scratcher – bed – until about twelve noon, only getting up for the occasional cup of tea. Lunch is about two o'clock, not bad if it is rice and lamb, pretty dreadful if it is rice and fish, and downright lousy if it is beef.

We sleep late because we do not usually get to sleep until two in the morning or later.

Not knowing how long we would be imprisoned, I decided to try and make the best of it. I soon realised that there was no point in becoming agitated or upset by the turn of events and that the best way of coping would be to adopt the Muslim philosophy of fatalism, 'what will be, will be'. *Inshallah!* As God wills!

I was strongly influenced by my mother, a Quaker, when it came to any religious beliefs. I incline very strongly to the concepts of Quakerism, that there is a little of God in everyone, that you don't actually need to go to church or do any formal things to be Christian or religious. It is just a matter of doing the right thing really, of following your own 'inner light'. I believe that kept me sane and prompted me to get something positive out of this whole prison episode.

Having done nothing that I considered to be a crime, I was not weighed down by guilt and so I determined to make the most of the experience. In a way I had been given the opportunity for an unaccustomed but useful time for reflection and introspection, not usually compatible with professional life. And in a small way I began to grasp something of the experience of so many of Africa's rulers who have gone on to become great leaders after having been in prison.

How ironic that incarceration, a feared punishment, brought with it rich rewards. However, no matter how hard I tried to keep myself occupied and to keep my spirits up, I knew deep within me, these were all mere distractions. There was one question that was always foremost in my mind.

What was happening with our case?

It must have been a few days after we were moved to the main prison that we were taken to the office and shown statements, written in Arabic with an English translation.

'Read and sign them,' we were told. The statements were placed together in piles. Four or five of our group had similar ones. Penny's and Tim's were different from the rest.

My statement admitted that I had hosted the party for Tim, at which alcohol had been served and women present, and that I had had a drink. That was it. The entire statement was based around these facts. There was no mention of Helen Smith or Johannes Otten.

Statements of the others acknowledged that the Germans and Jacques had attended a party at which alcohol had been served, but they had not drunk any. In truth, they had, of course, all drunk alcohol. But they had denied this when questioned by the police.

Tim and Penny's statements confirmed that they had been 'together' after the party at which there had been alcohol and dancing.

There was no mention of Helen Smith, Johannes Otten or their subsequent fate in any of the statements. What were we to make of this staggering omission? Was the strategy for the Saudi authorities to hold us on the party and alcohol charges while they investigated the deaths?

'We won't sign these until we have the translations independently verified,' I told the policemen present.

'Yes,' agreed Jacques, 'we don't know what the hell we are signing.'

A day or two later, we were interviewed again by Colonel Abdul el Garda and again given the statements to sign. This time we all dutifully signed the English version of the Arabic statement, realising that nothing would progress until we did, ignoring earlier advice to have this checked first.

On Wednesday 6 June, we were taken to the town court house, the *makhama*. I was dressed in the sarong I wore daily while in the prison. Penny and Tim's statements were read out, and signed, in the higher court. The rest of us went through the same procedure in the lower court.

There was no cross examination. Again the only points of interest were the party and the fact that there was alcohol and that there were women present. The papers were now to go to Prince Fawaz bin Abdul Aziz, the Governor of Mecca. Jeddah is in the Mecca Region. We were told he would make a decision as to our future in the next seven to fourteen days.

◻◿◻

Ours was a very sensitive case. Because it focused on the implications of immorality, a huge rumour mill started up in Saudi Arabia. This in turn was exacerbated by the enormous fuss made by the British press.

'We have heard that Ron Smith has a nine-page report on you,' Samir, the English-speaking detective, told me. That did not concern me so much as his following comment, that there were reports from the hospital about an apparent affair between myself and Helen Smith. From whom had such a rumour sprung?

'You are likely to be deported,' he told me on the journey back in the car.

'What about Penny?' I asked.

The prison governor had hinted to me that the inquiry into the two deaths was not finished. He had informed me that the authorities had developed a photograph which showed Helen and Tim together. What did that mean in Saudi eyes? That the two of them had been having a relationship? Perhaps, Penny, as the imagined other woman, cast doubts on the theory of accidental death?

'The Germans and Jacques?' I inquired of Samir.

'No, they will not be deported.' They would be able to resume their work and their lives.

A day or two later the members of our group were beginning to feel a bit down in the dumps, Tim especially. We had temporarily run out of books to read and I was waiting anxiously for a visit from Francis Geere.

When he came, he confirmed my worst fears.

'The whole emphasis of the case has been changed,' Geere told me at a meeting. Present also were Penny, Judy Hindle and Dr Bakhsh.

Geere looked sombre.

'What do you mean?'

'They are focusing on the alcohol at the party and the sex angle, rather than the two deaths.'

Penny grimaced. No one said anything but the thought that adultery was a capital offence was in all of our minds.

'The case has been passed from Prince Fawaz to the King in Riyadh,' Geere continued.

Our case was too big for the courts and even Prince Fawaz to handle, so it was being passed up the line to more and more important figures.

Dr Bakhsh coughed, 'I have spoken with the local chief of police. He told me that the case will certainly not be judged on sharia lines. It cannot be. You are not Muslims,' he said. Penny and I felt reassured for a short time until we learnt otherwise.

The Germans, however, were more fortunate. An embassy official visited them with the information that a German Foreign Office minister would come the following week and try to see Prince Fawaz, Governor of Mecca, on their behalf.

And so a pattern was set and our frustration continued, with promised action regularly coming to nothing. Official papers and documents were sent from office to office, around and around with no discernible results. There were rumours and snippets of news. We were given confusing and conflicting advice and constant misinformation. No one – not the British Embassy nor the prison authorities – knew at any given moment where our papers were or on whose desk they were sitting.

◰◱◲

THURSDAY 7 JUNE
Woke up at about 9.30 after a great sleep. Dreaming very clearly about being a ship's doctor again on the Cape Town Castle. As I woke up, the bustle and noise and music in the cell block was a bit like the activity on a ship with the shoreside fitters and cleaners before they leave. Unfortunately this lot are not going anywhere at present.

Chat with Tim – he was on the RMS Canberra, November 1966 Auckland to Sydney when I was the doctor.

◰◱◲

FRIDAY 8 JUNE
2 p.m. Diploma ceremony, Royal College of Surgeons, Edinburgh
8 p.m. Dinner, Black tie

Under this entry, which I had obviously made months ago, before my imprisonment, I wrote 'So sorry – unable to attend'. A black tie event in Scotland. A prestigious gathering of surgeons. A world and a lifetime away from me.

◰◱◲

TUESDAY 12 JUNE
Penny collapsed yesterday evening, very tired.

WEDNESDAY 13 JUNE

Penny visited flat yesterday with police, guards and Geere. They have changed the locks. Place thick with dust. Packed up children's things. Sent in some clothes and books for me. Didn't do much all day but slept much better last night.

The deputy-governor of the prison, Captain Saad, turns out to be a very pleasant fellow. A true Bedouin, he is of slim build with a trim moustache and a dazzling smile. Captain Saad let me go to the women's prison where I talked to Penny for about fifteen minutes. She is developing a nasty sinus infection and is feeling pretty rotten.

SATURDAY 16 JUNE

Tried to see Penny. No success. Expected a visit from Francis Geere but he did not appear. I seem to be developing an allergy to the bedding here and I am sneezing badly. Have had some bronchospasm at night. Nothing serious so far.

MONDAY 18 JUNE

Bad night with asthma. Didn't sleep a wink.

I persuaded Captain Saad to let me return to the flat to pick up a Ventolin inhaler I had there. At the flat I packed everything in the children's room which was to be locked.

The empty whisky bottles we had stowed away on top of the cupboard before the police came were still there, undisturbed. The police had obviously not found them. I brought back a few items to the prison with me – some books, board games and children's toys.

I was also allowed to visit the hospital, where I had quite an emotional reception. Dr Bakhsh confirmed there would still be a job for me unless I got blacklisted. He said that he supported me but not Penny.

My mind raced back to Penny's first meeting with Dr Bakhsh in London. That seemed a lifetime ago now. Remember how Penny had not trusted Dr Bakhsh and now, bearing in mind his lack of support for her, it was apparent that the dislike and mistrust was mutual.

回己回

WEDNESDAY 20 JUNE
Chap in bed next to me is in leg irons because of fighting.

With time on my hands in prison, I thought long and hard about my marriage. I decided to tell Penny the next time I saw her that I was not prepared to ruin both of our lives. I scribbled down a few notes in my diary: 'If she wants out, so be it. If she wants to stay . . . Realise that perhaps what is lacking is interest.'

I sent a note to Captain Saad, the prison deputy-governor, requesting to see Penny. My application was put aside for the day as a great squad of people from all prison sections with chickenpox were rounded up for smallpox inoculations. The medical rationale behind this was somewhat puzzling to me. Were they terrified a misdiagnosis had been made? Were they therefore inoculating against smallpox just to be on the safe side?

I slept well that night, apart from the rattle of fetters. The man beside me, chained and manacled, had every move accompanied with a clatter and jangle.

In the morning, I went to Captain Saad's office. By a coincidence, Penny had also written to him requesting a visit. Captain Saad took this to be an official husband and wife visit in the local knocking room. (The Arabs, whom we regard as puritanical, at least have an unofficial system of conjugal visits for married prisoners.)

回己回

THURSDAY 21 JUNE
There seems to be an awful lot of bronchitis and asthma among the prisoners, also a lot of TB. Must have an X-ray when I get out.

Chief Muslim gave the faithful one hell of a wigging yesterday —
sounded like fire and brimstone. In fact he was telling them not to
block the loos with soap and paper.

◧己◨

MONDAY 25 JUNE
Got back in time to meet Francis, Judy Hindle, Penny and the
children in Saad's office — not Sunday.
    Kissed the kids goodbye — they are looking forward to getting
their bikes.

'Look, here are some of your toys,' and I handed Lucy her doll and
William some of his model cars I had managed to salvage from the
flat.

'When are you coming to England?' asked William.

'Very soon,' I promised.

'Come with us now, Daddy,' pleaded Lucy in a quavering voice.

'I would love to but I have a few things to sort out here. Mummy
and I will come to England very soon. And you'll have fun there,
with Grandma.'

'And the new bikes!'

'Yes, and the new bikes.' I kissed them goodbye.

After they left, I asked Francis Geere how the case was going.

'Nothing to report, Richard.'

'This is just dragging on. When will you have something to tell
me?'

'Who can say? I'm doing my best.'

'Are you? Nothing seems to be happening.'

'You have to be patient.'

'I am being very patient but my patience is running out. It's been
over a month and we're now in gaol with no end in sight. Apart
from anything else, we haven't been charged with any crime.'

'Do you expect special treatment?'

'I just expect some treatment and some action,' I fumed.

Tuesday 26 June

Woken at 7 a.m. for count. Repeated five times in the morning, twice at night and once next morning. Apparently there are 201 prisoners in the block – should only be 200. The little Malay gold dealer has gone into a complete decline and lies on the tiled floor day and night. The guards do not disturb him. A day or two ago I noticed his face was swollen.

Wednesday 27 June

Kids flew back to England today. Germans visited by their embassy and Harms Salvage people. Bad news. Our case seems to be absolutely static; nothing is happening. They and the Brits got in touch for the first time a week ago. German papers still talking about our case.

What keeps me going are the letters I receive from family and friends. Although these are not delivered to me for some time, they bring me comfort and joy as well as news when I finally do get to read them.

I was touched that former patients, on hearing of my plight through the British newspapers, made the effort to write to me. Friends and colleagues with whom I had lost contact for many years suddenly got in touch and longtime acquaintances wrote extensive letters.

Sometimes the news, while keeping me in touch, was not so good. One letter gave details of Ron Smith, 'Judging by the report in today's *Daily Mail*, Mr Smith's claims are becoming more and more ridiculous – allegations of conspiracy and sophisticated plots to murder Helen.'

My blood boiled. As if it was not hot enough already. That day the mercury reached 49 degrees Celcius (120 degrees in the old measure).

MONDAY 25 JUNE

Surprise, surprise! — called at 9.30 a.m. by Samir — Jacques and I have to go to the court to witness the judge signing our statements which he had omitted to do 3 weeks ago. Christ! what a waste of time.

I was called to the office first thing in the morning. I was greeted by the detective, Samir. Good, some action at last.

'What news do you have for me?' I asked.

'You and Jacques have to go to the court.'

'Why?'

'To witness the judge signing your statements.'

'But we were there three weeks ago with the statements! Why did he not sign them then?'

What a waste of time. Samir assured me that the papers would go to the Governor of Mecca the following day.

I had my doubts.

◨◩◧

My time in prison was made bearable by the prison library. It was only after I had been incarcerated for some time that I was allowed to visit the library. It was a small room, perhaps even smaller than our cell. A single table stood in the middle of the room; around that were a few chairs. It was there that I applied myself to the Arabic-English dictionary, studying to improve my skills in the written language in which there are no vowels, only consonants.

The books were mainly Arabic titles, but there were also English books from a previous British prisoner who had been caught some years earlier with hashish in his car. Jeddah's British community had brought him in presents and books, which he had left behind on his release. How grateful I was for them now.

For short periods of time, I left the heat of the Middle East behind me and escaped, immersing myself in a world of fantasy. I left my troubles and concerns and journeyed to the animal kingdom of *Watership Down*, travelled to England of the last century in *Until the Colours Fade* and modern day Africa in *The Sparrow Falls* by Wilbur Smith. I read Mary Renault's historical novels and books by Nevil Shute, Nigel Balchin and Alan Moorehead. *Disputed Passage* by Lloyd Douglas told of the wartime romance between an American surgeon and a Chinese woman and was a particular favourite of mine.

Other books had more of a profound impact on me. I noted parts of them that held special significance for me in my diary.

Sir William Stephenson's account of his time as head of the British Secret Service, *A Man called Intrepid*, included some memorable quotes. Duff Cooper's words from 1938 carried particular relevance for me: 'I have ruined perhaps my political career but that is a little matter. I have retained something which is to me of great value – I can still walk about the world with my head erect.'

Then there were the words chosen for the speech of King George VI in 1939: 'I said to the man at the gate of the year – "Give me a light that I may tread safely into the unknown". And he replied, "Go out into the darkness and put your hand into the hand of God. That shall be to you better than light and safer than a known way". . . may that almighty hand guide and uphold us all.' These words have helped to sustain me ever since.

In the library, too, I learnt more of Saudi Arabia's history. Founded by Abdul Aziz Ibn Saud, the Kingdom of Saudi Arabia is the only country in the world to be named after a family or clan.

Abdul Aziz Ibn Saud was born in 1880. In 1902, he and his followers captured Riyadh from its Rashidi occupiers. Campaigning against other rulers across the Arabian peninsula, he waged war, made alliances and married over three hundred times until becoming the King of the Hijaz in 1925. The Hijaz and other regions he captured later were officially unified as the Kingdom of Saudi Arabia in 1932.

An undeveloped and impoverished nation, its fortunes changed dramatically six years later, when Aramco, the Arabian-American Oil Company, found the world's largest oil field there, one-third of the world's reserves. Saudi Arabia became the world's leading producer and exporter of oil. Within a few decades, this feudal kingdom at the crossroads of Europe, Africa and Asia was flourishing. Nevertheless reticulated electricity did not come until 1960 and slavery survived into the 1960s.

Abdul Aziz Ibn Saud, who died in 1953, had about fifty sons and over 250 daughters, resulting in at least two thousand Saudi princes. Counting up all the branches, the males of the Saudi royal family comprise over 4000 in number. Many of them are in the Saudi government and armed forces.

Abdul Aziz Ibn Saud was succeeded by his son of the same name, who is generally known now merely as Ibn Saud. His regime was corrupt and short lived. He soon lost the right to govern, and the throne itself was handed to his brother Faisal by the Saud family and the *ulama* or holy men in 1964. Ibn Saud died in exile in Athens. Faisal ruled until he was assassinated in 1975. King Khalid, younger brother of Faisal, then succeeded to the throne.

◧◩◧

Being a surgeon made no difference to my situation or status in the prison, except when it came to my expertise. My case was not rushed through, nor was I given preferential treatment.

It was my being a foreigner, rather than a medical professional, that gave me prestige and standing in prison. More than once I was impressed by the courtesy shown me. On one occasion, I was in a crowd, waiting to fill my bucket with water when the young Saudi in front of me took it and, saying '*gawaja*', filled it for me. A Pakistani objected, saying that he was a *gawaja* – foreigner – as well. But he was overruled. Those who had come to Saudi Arabia from countries such as Pakistan and the Philippines to provide cheap manual labour were treated as third-class citizens.

The days went by slowly but I didn't feel particularly sorry for myself. I felt angry rather than depressed. I felt angry at being imprisoned although I had had nothing to do with the deaths. I felt angry that people like Dr Bakhsh and others did not give me more support. And I felt angry that, when word got out about Penny and Tim's little fling, I was tarred by that brush. There wasn't a lot that I could do about that so I just had to wear it.

It may seem a curious thing to say, but I almost feel that people who haven't been through a prison experience as I have, have missed out on something. Terrible as they were, those few months really changed me as a person. I found that I came to adopt exactly the same attitude to people, regardless of who they were, where they came from, what they did. I tended to treat people purely on their merits, not taking anything else into account. They were all exactly the same as far as I was concerned.

回凸回

I was surprised to discover Morris, the Palestinian, was a Christian, unusual in itself in this part of the world but even more unexpected in view of his behaviour.

'You pray with the others. I thought you were a Muslim, Morris.'

'Yes,' he smiled, 'it is easier that way, to pray with them and let them think I am a Muslim.' Morris also taught me the importance of self-respect, and, even more importantly, respect for others.

The daily program of prayer in this wing is pretty gruelling. Prayers are one of the most significant practices of Islam. Broadly, a Muslim's prayers are to be offered five times a day. The faithful are woken for the first *salah* soon after 3.30 in the morning, for the 4.00 a.m. prayers. After that, there is reading and a general buzz of conversation. Prayers follow then at mid-morning, at lunchtime, at 6.00, and then 8.00 p.m. (Noon prayers on Friday are most important.)

Each prayer time, the central corridor and even some of the cells are cleared. The prayers are performed in an established way. After ritual washing, the worshipper bows, kneels, prostrates himself (or presumably herself), and at the same time speaks words proclaiming the glory of God. It is like living in a mosque and I find it a good opportunity to observe the praying. Some people in here are intensely religious, reading the Koran and chanting most of the time.

The prayers are led by a succession of *sayedis*, 'wise men'. It appears to be completely ritualised and formalised, the followers chanting and joining in together at exactly the right moment. To me, it appears to have almost a drug-like or soporific effect. While chanting, the faithful seem almost in a trance.

The chief prayer man in our wing is Egyptian. He is serving a fifteen-year sentence for drugs. Sometimes he comes close to being assaulted by some of the others because he is not a Saudi.

◨◪◨

I continued to take the attitude that the only way for me to survive in prison was to make the best of my situation. I tried to get the most out of every incident, like getting to know the Arab prisoners, really getting to know them. Once I was able to communicate with them, albeit with basic skills, I began to learn humility from them. No matter how bad some of them appeared at first, there was an interesting side to the person if you took the trouble to listen.

◨◪◨

The foul conditions here could break the spirit. The treatment that was handed out to us could further break that spirit. Locked in cells though we were, on the rare occasions that we left the prison confines, we were always chained hand and foot. I felt degraded and humiliated.

'Handcuffs,' the guards would demand. We were never taken out anywhere without wearing handcuffs. I found them particularly demeaning. At first I accepted the situation. Then I decided I would stand for it no longer. For, slowly, I was getting back my self-esteem.

From time to time, my teeth gave me pain. I put up with the discomfort for as long as I could, unwilling to face the lengthy and tedious process of obtaining permission and stamps of authorisation before being allowed to leave the prison, under guard, to visit the dentist.

On one occasion, when my toothache was unbearable, I was finally granted approval for treatment. 'You will go to the Bab Sharif Hospital.'

What? The conditions were appalling at the general hospital.

'No.' I stood up for myself. 'I want to see Dr Wilkinson at the Bakhsh Hospital.'

After some discussion, Captain Saad agreed. He left, and I was led away. By now, I was worn out by the rigmarole, but not too exhausted to make a final stand.

'No,' I snapped, to the consternation of the guards. 'No, I am not wearing handcuffs,' I told them.

'No, I'm not wearing handcuffs,' I repeated. A dreadful fuss ensued. Eventually Captain Saad was called back. He had asked me for a few favours in the past, medical advice for his family and so forth. Now it was my turn to appeal to him for help. The Saudis were very concerned about maintaining face and, at the same time, showing respect.

'I don't want to wear handcuffs,' I told him.

He stared at me in surprise. No prisoner ever left the gaol without handcuffs.

'Look, there is nowhere for me to run,' I pointed out. 'I'm not going to try to escape,' I continued, ' I'm only going to the hospital where I used to work.'

That it was indeed the hospital, and my former place of employment to which I was going, had unnerved me. What I was really saying was that wearing handcuffs to my previous workplace was too much of a personal humiliation. The last time I had been to the hospital, for a chest X-ray, I had had to stand with my manacled hands raised above my head while the X-ray was taken.

Captain Saad turned to the guards and issued his instructions that I could walk hands-free through the prison to the vehicle that was to take me to the hospital. A small victory perhaps, but a large one for my self-esteem and a big boost to my confidence.

◧◪◨

The days passed. Frustration built up once more as no progress seemed to be being made in our case. Then came a glimmer of light. Francis Geere mentioned the possibility that we could be released from gaol 'under guarantee'.

'Is that a house arrest situation?'

'Similar. You are released under the guarantee of your sponsors or embassy. You would be able to leave the house, but naturally not the country, until the case has been resolved.'

That sounded far preferable to our present situation. Yet the days passed and we heard nothing. Confusion reigned as more snippets of information came from other sources. The Harms Salvage company telexed their head office in Hamburg, to keep them in touch with our plight. The Germans in the prison with me found out what was said.

'An informant has let Harms Salvage know that the investigating police believe the last people left the party at 4.00 a.m. and not 3.30 a.m.,' one of the Germans told me. 'That means the big case is not settled,' he went on.

'But I thought the police were satisfied the deaths were accidental and we were being held on the social crimes, the alcohol and the women present.'

The German shrugged his shoulders. 'Also they do not know anything about an intention to release us under guarantee, and the Governor of Mecca is in Europe.'

'So nothing happens until he returns? Doesn't his deputy have the power to take over in his absence?'

Everyone told us a different story – the British Embassy, the Saudis, the people at the prison. Now this telex confounded matters even more. Crossed and conflicting messages formed a jumbled and bewildering picture which led us nowhere.

'For goodness sake, we've been here nine weeks now and it was an accident. We've paid enough of a penalty for this party,' I fumed.

Apart from such occasions, we never talked about the party between ourselves. There was no point. What did we have to discuss? We had not been responsible for the deaths of Helen Smith or Johannes Otten. We were not the types to mull over that evening's events, feeling sorry for ourselves. A tragic accident had occurred and we now had to deal with its ramifications.

Did I think of those who had died while I was in prison?

I did.

I felt sorrow at their untimely demise and sympathy for their families and loved ones. I did not know Johannes, having met him for the first time the night of the party, but I thought of Helen.

I re-directed my irritation to Dr Bakhsh. I wrote a letter, asking him to liaise with the British Embassy and find out what was happening. Bakhsh was my sponsor, after all, and should be taking care of such matters.

◨🀰◧

SUNDAY 1 JULY

My visits with Penny continue to bring mixed blessings. When she is feeling well and in good spirits, as she was today, we get on well. She had just had a shower and was feeling refreshed, although very cut off. We had a good chat and she was more cheerful by the time she left. She has decided to try and get the use of one of the prison offices so she can write and do some needlework. Anything that gives her slightly more comfortable surroundings and an interest would be extremely beneficial.

My mood was good that day and I even tried a little bit of humour to lift her spirits and to let her know that all was not doom and gloom, that perhaps we could be reconciled. I would forgive and forget.

'What's a bit of adultery between friends?' I joked.

◰◳◰

Thursdays and Sundays are Ruwais prison visiting days. It is no small event. Hundreds of visitors clamber to get in.

This is not England, with people queuing and politely waiting to take their turn to enter. Here, throngs of people push and shove their way forward.

Women, rather than men, of the immediate family – mothers and sisters – visit the male Arab prisoners. Because Arab males dress similarly in long white *thobe*s and head dresses, people sometimes exchange identities and prisoners walk out to freedom in place of the visitor.

Western women friends and acquaintances were allowed to visit the Western male prisoners. Pip Reddaway and Sharon Parmenter, whose husbands worked at the Australian Embassy, were frequent visitors. Although I had only met them briefly before the fateful party, they proved to be wonderfully supportive and visited regularly each week.

'It was hideous out there today, a huge scrum, absolutely awful,' said Pip. Looking distressed, she wiped the sweat from her face. It was a particularly hot afternoon.

'Everyone was jostling; people were trying to get into the shade; others were trying to get in the gate and a woman was actually pushed to the ground and trampled to death,' added Sharon softly. 'The crowd trampled her to death, Richard.'

We sat in silence for a few seconds, in shock and disbelief.

Finally Pip spoke. 'Have you had any news, Richard?'

'No,' I replied despondently, 'there seems to be no progress in our case.' I paused, thinking of the Nigerian who had been here for years, lost in the system. 'Perhaps they have forgotten about us.' I managed a wry smile.

'Of course they haven't,' said Sharon, 'it's just that things take a little longer here.' How right she was.

回己回

SUNDAY 8 JULY

Better night. Slept right through to 9.30 — 8 hours. Jean and Angela de Klee visited. Angela, whose husband is the British military attaché, says we are mentioned almost every day at the Ambassador's prayer session.

回己回

FRIDAY 20 JULY

Did not sleep too well.

In the morning, my bucket of cold water had gone. Like all the other prisoners, I left a bucket to cool overnight for my morning wash. Someone had pinched it. Furious, I took someone else's. As I was about to wash, Said suddenly went berserk and attacked me. With meanness written all over him, Said slugged me in the face. With no hesitation, I punched him back. Two buckets of water were spilt over the bedding in the ensuing melee. It happened so quickly no one had a chance to intervene, and I emerged with a black eye.

But standing up for myself proved to be a moral victory. Fighting was forbidden in prison. The punishment for brawls was to be put into manacles. The Saudis did not like violence and were very quick to break up a fight. As soon as any physical confrontation started to develop, everyone would jump in and quickly separate the combatants.

Doctor in prison

At the age of ten or eleven I had my first lesson in racism. It was one I was never to forget.

We were living in Rhodesia at the time. I was shopping with my mother and needed help to carry a box of groceries. I turned to one of the African packers in the store and imperiously commanded, 'Boy, come and carry this box for me.' Everyone knew blacks were servants.

But this time, something different happened. The man said gravely, 'How can a small boy like you call a grown man like me, old enough to be your grandfather, "boy"?'

I was shocked. This had never happened to me before. I did not know what to say. Utterly confused, I rephrased my demand to a polite request. And, for the first time in my life, I began to realise what racism is all about.

Later, when I was reading medicine at the University of St Andrews in Scotland with black students from Ghana and Nigeria, I felt that we Rhodesians, although branded as racists after Ian Smith's Unilateral Declaration of Independence, got on far better with our African peers than did our non-African colleagues.

Over the long months in Ruwais, I enjoyed sharing my medical knowledge with Saudi inmates and officials alike. My medical skills were often called upon by my fellow prisoners and sometimes by the guards.

A few days after entering gaol I asked, and was permitted, to visit the prison clinic. I was horrified by what I saw. The conditions were basic. The pharmacy was stocked with masses of vitamins, cough medicines and antibiotics, all in a terrible muddle. The whole place was a shambles and the clinic seemed to be full of malingerers and neurotics. The job must have been pretty soul-destroying for the two part-time Egyptian staff doctors.

Dr Abbas, one of the clinic doctors, was a kind and friendly man who wanted to work in England and hoped that I might help him. He invited me to attend to some of the clinic patients. Most of that first batch were suffering from various aches and coughs, as well as *tabaab* – that is, tiredness, fatigue.

The next time I visited, I examined a few patients suffering from chest complaints and saw an amazing case of a badly healed arm.

'You look as if you have two elbows on your right arm,' I told the patient, who was from Yemen. He grimaced. The poor fellow had broken his arm in a motor vehicle accident for which he had been arrested and flung into prison.

'The doctor said there was nothing to worry about,' the Yemeni told me. As a faithful Muslim, he then made the best of it. The result of the chronic malunion of the humerus was an extra joint in his upper arm.

The prison clinic was not up to much, but it was not the first time I had been disappointed with a Jeddah hospital. The Bakhsh Hospital had been a great letdown, too. When I first saw that, my heart sank. What had I let myself in for? Why had I abandoned my career in England and uprooted my entire life and family? The exterior scaffolding was still in place. There appeared to be ages of work still to be done. The area surrounding the hospital was a mass of trenches, piles of sand and builders' rubble.

Although our new hospital looked many months from completion when we arrived, the American contractors worked at an amazing pace. Building had begun only ten months previously. A large basement hole had been rapidly excavated and the kitchens, X-ray department, operating theatre, gynaecological suite and utility area, boilers and maintenance laid out in ferroconcrete. The ground floor, which comprised the administrative area, outpatients, casualty department, pharmacy and pathology lab were similarly outlined in ferroconcrete on to which the prefabricated wall panels were fixed. Then came the clever part. The top three floors of patients' rooms and offices had been entirely prefabricated as complete units in Texas and shipped to Saudi Arabia in crates. They were unpacked and simply hoisted into position by a large crane, just like a set of outsize children's blocks, and slotted into the ferroconcrete structure.

Water, electrical and telephone lines were then joined up. After the roof was in place, it was merely a matter of interior and exterior decorating details. Shortly, the scaffolding was removed and the rubble cleared.

So, soon after we arrived towards the end of November the finishing details were completed, inside and out. During the next weeks we unpacked thousands of boxes of medical equipment, supplies and stores.

The Bakhsh Hospital opened its doors on 17 January 1979, short of some supplies and unable to use the operating theatres for anything but the most minor surgery. But at least we were open. Our first patients probably came more out of curiosity than because of our reputation.

Three other general surgeons, two from Lebanon and one from Egypt were to work in my department. The Egyptian surgeon had been an associate professor in Cairo. It was interesting to find the so-called British medical staff consisted entirely of myself, Frank Vernon, the gynaecologist, Ian Keith, the anaesthetist, and Kit Wilkinson, the dentist. Everyone else was Saudi, Egyptian, Malaysian, Pakistani or Maltese.

The 'all British nursing staff' too was a slight exaggeration, there being only seven from England. The rest were Jamaican or Malaysian. They had all, however, been trained in England or Malaysia which uses the British system and seemed a competent lot.

The entire hospital staff comprised some fifty or so individuals, the average number for a hospital in the area. As the only hospital in Jeddah with a high complement of British medical and nursing staff, the place quickly became busy. Within the first week, I was seeing up to twenty patients a day, right across the surgical spectrum: hernias, breast lumps, duodenal ulcers and kidney stones. The hours were long but the work interesting and so, for six days a week, I attended to the surgical misfortunes of the local population.

Competition between hospitals for patients in Jeddah was intense. In early 1978, there were five private hospitals, one government hospital and one military hospital. A year later, two more private clinics had been completed, another five were nearing completion and more were planned. A brand new government hospital was due to open shortly.

The window-dressing aspect of my appointment, and that of the other three British staff: Frank, Ian and Kit was that we were there to reassure the populace that they would be treated according to British ethical principles. Foreign doctors and Western-trained Arab and Egyptian doctors had a definite cachet in Saudi Arabia compared with the Egyptian and Palestinian doctors who staffed the government clinics. Many expatriates flocked to our doors in view of the British connection and we soon became known as the British Bakhsh Hospital. In 1979, I was the only British surgeon working in Saudi Arabia. All the other private hospitals in Jeddah at that time were staffed by American, Egyptian or Arab doctors, with nurses coming from Malaysia, Egypt or the Philippines. Our British image also attracted many patients from the large, shifting expatriate population of engineers and building contractors and their families.

Yet things did not altogether run smoothly. My planned department never really got off the ground which was a pity as there was nothing in Jeddah at that time approaching the standard of treatment and care we could have provided. I had a clear idea as to how the new department of surgery would run. Dr Bakhsh had told me he wanted his hospital organised on the lines of a British hospital. He had spent two years in London working as a senior house officer in urology and had developed a great admiration for the style of British hospital medicine.

One of the difficulties with private medicine, and especially surgery, in many parts of the world is that ethical values are often overtaken by financial values resulting in much unnecessary intervention. This was partly the reason why surgery in the Middle East had gained a bad reputation and why patients travelled to medical centres in Europe and America for an opinion about their fate.

I was quite prepared to send some patients to London, where I had excellent contacts in all branches of surgery. While this doubtless meant losing those patients, I considered that once the hospital established a reputation for safe and honest surgery, the policy would more than pay for itself in the increased referral of surgical cases from general practitioners. Dr Bakhsh assured me that he fully agreed.

However, notwithstanding our good intentions, practising medicine in Jeddah was full of surprises. One afternoon, at the Bakhsh Hospital, a group of women entered, one of them to be my patient. She entered my consulting room, followed by her entourage. My secretary, Leila, introduced her as a princess.

All of the women were clothed in head-to-toe *abaya*s. Most also had the face completely covered with veils. The princess wore a total of five veils. The more veils a woman wore, the more modest she was considered.

'I have found a lump in my breast,' the princess told me through an interpreter.

After taking her medical history, I told her I needed to carry out an examination. Keeping her veils on, the princess removed her top clothes so that I could examine her breast and under her armpit.

'Yes, I can feel the lump,' I told her. 'It is probably an infected sweat gland and will have to be removed surgically.'

'Where should this be done?' she asked.

'Here of course, in the operating theatre,' I told her, explaining that it would be a relatively minor operation. Instantly an excited discussion began among the women.

'It is not possible to do it here. We have to go somewhere else,' I was told.

'Where?' I asked, somewhat puzzled.

'Paris perhaps, London maybe or Chicago.'

It was only much later that I realised this was the only opportunity these women had for any sort of freedom; to travel out of Saudi Arabia on any sort of pretext. A medical reason, such as this, would allow them to spend some weeks away from the confines of Jeddah.

◨◪◨

My particular interest in surgery is gastroenterology and there lay one frustration. Modern gastroenterology had, at that time, been revolutionised by the flexible fibreoptic endoscope, a pliable instrument which, when inserted into the upper gastrointestinal tract, enabled the doctor to look directly into a person's stomach. Dr Bakhsh had assured me that a complete range of endoscopes was waiting at the hospital. However, when the boxes of medical equipment were opened, not one was to be found. The instruments were only delivered five months later, just three weeks before the fateful party and the premature end of my surgical career in Saudi Arabia. Nevertheless, despite the absence of the endoscopes, I was able to practise and I dealt with some fascinating problems.

Surgical practice in Jeddah was interesting and varied. Without a doubt, my favourite patients were Bedouin. They had a far better understanding of physiology and the basic disease process than the average British patient and tended to be stoical. Rarely was I bothered by hypochondriacal or neurotic Bedouin patients. Furthermore, they were very grateful for often quite minor medical treatment and I was often overwhelmed by their generosity and hospitality.

One such was Sheikh Ali, a tough old Bedouin in his sixties. He had been brought 400 kilometres by his sons to see me, the 'English doctor'. He had developed a large upper abdominal swelling over the past two years which had begun to worry him. It was relatively painless and caused him little discomfort but it was steadily getting bigger.

When I examined him, I found a large firm but smooth swelling in his liver which moved easily as he breathed. I suspected it might be a hydatid cyst of the liver, a common cause of abdominal swelling in the rural parts of Saudi Arabia. An X-ray showed the typical eggshell calcification lying in the liver and the diagnosis was almost certain.

'This is a major operation,' I warned his sons, 'and it is potentially dangerous.'

They accepted my words with typical Islamic equanimity. '*Inshallah, Inshallah*,' they told me, 'as Allah wills.'

I embarked on four hours of difficult surgery, cutting away the cyst and part of the liver. The cyst had eroded into a large hepatic bile duct and the common bile duct and gall bladder were stuffed with daughter cysts. Carefully I removed as much of the debris as I could before joining the bile duct to the duodenum.

The old man withstood the long and taxing operation and several days of severe post-operative discomfort without turning a hair. His twenty-three sons came to visit him in relays, all insisting on seeing the enormous specimen I had removed and which now lay in a bucket of formalin.

What struck me most was that, for those first five days, Sheikh Ali was invariably awake, no matter what time of day or night I visited. He lay there quietly, various draining tubes attached to his body, never once complaining about the pain or discomfort. By about the seventh day he was doing famously, eating well and in good spirits. His only complaint was that his sons refused to fetch his guns. He felt naked without them. I was amazed and delighted at the manner of his rapid recovery. He returned home a fortnight after the operation and, sadly, I was never to see him again. By the time he returned for his first post-operative visit, I was imprisoned.

Some of the affluent non-Bedouin patients were another story altogether: neurotic, demanding and struck down by imaginary ailments, the sort of patients who make a doctor's life a misery.

However, I found my job in the Bakhsh Hospital was becoming

difficult. Despite an increasingly busy practice, I found that I could not rely on the resident doctors who should have been responsible for routine inpatient work – the general physical examination, taking of clinical history, blood tests and X-rays. I found I had to do everything myself. Even the simplest and most basic post-operative care had to be personally supervised in order to avoid unnecessary danger, pain or discomfort to the patient.

After four months, I was spending up to seventy hours a week at the hospital. The work was demanding and I was at work ten to twelve hours a day, six days a week. Despite these problems, I thoroughly enjoyed practice in Jeddah.

As well as my work at the Bakhsh Hospital, I was part-time consultant surgeon to a downmarket sister hospital, the Dar al Shifa, where I had to deal with a lot of fascinating medical problems. At first, language was a great problem as many of the patients spoke no English. But, stimulated by a dislike of working through interpreters, I soon picked up enough basic Arabic to manage largely unaided. The least effort by a *gawaja* to speak Arabic is greeted by great delight and enthusiasm and it was very rewarding. Later, learning some Arabic and working in a less salubrious environment turned out to be very useful experience.

◻◿◻

Work in the prison clinic had its rewards, too. Dr Abbas often provided me with a roast chicken snack and allowed me to snooze for a little while in the luxurious air-conditioned comfort of the pharmacy before sending me back to my cell. Sometimes, on a very hot Friday, after noon prayers, he would invite me over for lunch. That was usually followed by a nap on the cool tiled floor of the dispensary.

One evening, a cry of 'Here, gawaja, here Dr Gawaja,' came from one of the prisoners. I was summoned to the *amaliad*, the office, by a guard. He came up to the barred gate of our cell block and called

—122—

out for me. The word had been spread from inmate to inmate until the message reached me.

I was to go to the *amaliad* to see Captain Saad. Did this mean there was news for me? A sudden shiver of anticipation and anxiety charged through me. I hastily made my way to the office.

When I rushed in, there was a guard standing next to Captain Saad.

'Good evening, doctor,' said the captain. 'This man has a favour to ask you. He has had a lot of pain and the doctor at the hospital has taken some X-rays.'

'Please, can you tell me, what does this mean?' asked the guard, handing over an X-ray. Immediately my tension faded to a slight feeling of deflation. I composed myself and concentrated intently on the radiograph.

'I have kidney stones,' the guard told me.

I accompanied him back to his post in the prison courtyard where I interpreted his intravenous pyelogram by the only available light, that of the moon. Out in the courtyard, it was a warm balmy evening and the moon was almost full. It shed a light almost as clear as daylight. I held up his X-ray and pointed, 'Look, here is a ureteric stone, there are the kidney stones.' The films clearly showed stones in both kidneys and the swollen ureter on the left side. A piece of that stone had broken off and was causing a blockage.

Kidney stones were endemic among the Arab population and particularly among the Bedouins. Drinking little fluid in such a hot climate, resulted in their urine becoming extremely concentrated. They might only pass a small amount daily. Consequently, dissolved substances in the urine tended to crystallise out and kidney stones were very common. And when the stones left the kidney and travelled down the ureter, if they lodged there, the blockage caused severe pain.

While we talked in the warm moonlight of the guard's medical condition, we drank hot sweet black tea from short glasses. I thought how exotic the setting of the consultation had turned out to be, but quite delightful.

The next day was a distressing one as I met other prisoners and considered their desperate plight. They helped me to forget my own troubles for a while.

Peter de Cito, a forty-five-year-old English-Italian had been accused of theft and incarcerated. He had spent eight days in manacles at the Sharifia before I met him. He had had a particularly hard time and his future looked bleak, but not only because of his legal troubles. He had been suffering from 'laryngitis' for the past ten weeks.

'The doctor gave me some antibiotics and cough medicine,' Peter told me.

'Did he examine your vocal cords?' I asked.

'No.'

It turned out Peter had a cancer of the vocal cords. When he eventually did get medical treatment, it came too late. He was moved to a hospital in the nearby city of Taif and had a biopsy a few days later. He almost certainly had final stage cancer of the larynx, with local extension and lung secondaries.

At the same time, Klaus Ritter was feeling very weak and tired. His appetite was poor and he was urinating frequently.

'You may be diabetic,' I told him, glancing at his obese figure. 'I'll need to test whether you have any sugar in your urine.' We went to the clinic and waited in vain for a couple of hours to see Dr Abbas.

Back in the block, still untreated and undiagnosed, Klaus became even more unwell. His temperature shot up to 42 degrees and he stopped sweating.

'This is really serious,' I told the others. Klaus was suffering from severe heatstroke. If his body temperature was not lowered promptly, he could die.

Klaus was soon moved to another section where they had air conditioning. Within twenty-four hours, he was feeling fine and had stopped passing lots of urine. Tests later showed he had normal blood sugar, hence no diabetes. His symptoms were probably due to heat intolerance.

The incident with Klaus encouraged me to carry out a medical study on fluid intake in the blistering climate of Jeddah. For a day I noted my own fluid intake and output. This was: 11.30 a.m. – 800 mL lemon juice; 5 p.m. – 750 mL Pepsi/juice; 7.15 p.m. – 500 mL Pepsi; 11.15 p.m. – 500 mL lemon juice; 11.55 p.m. – 500 mL lemon juice; 10.30 a.m. – 1200 mL lemon juice. My totals were: fluid intake that day, 4250 mL and output, 450 mL.

I was intrigued to discover just how much fluid one needed in that environment. I had sweat out nearly four litres of perspiration on that day. Next day I drank 3100 mL, peed 250 mL, and the following day's intake was 2800 mL with output of 600 mL. I had discovered I needed three to four litres a day just to lose in perspiration. That is an enormous amount. But, unless you drank that sort of volume in that environment, your urine would get terribly concentrated, and you would end up with kidney stones.

My own health suffered in Ruwais. Although I gained all sorts of mental and spiritual benefits from being a prisoner, physically I deteriorated. My hair went completely grey during my imprisonment. I became very weak and debilitated. I lost several kilograms in weight.

I suffered from minor medical problems while in prison: a severe asthma attack, chest pain, bouts of severe toothache. Eventually, I developed a large and painful swelling on the left side of my scrotum. Locked in the mental confinement of prison, I imagined I had a nasty cancer of the testicle.

I requested that I be allowed to consult a doctor and I saw my friend Terry Bennett, a Jeddah GP, and friend, who, as it turned out, had never drained one of these before. I told him how to insert the local anaesthetic and subsequently the needle in order to drain the hydrocele. Fortunately, it proved not to be a cancer of the testicle and I felt extremely relieved and much more comfortable afterwards.

Fasting and Freedom

To Westerners, if they have heard of it, Ramadan means the time when Muslims fast. In fact, the obligation to observe Ramadan is one of the five pillars of Islam; the others are the declaration of faith, daily prayers, giving alms to the poor, and making the Hajj (the pilgrimage to the Sacred Mosque at Mecca).

Ramadan commemorates God's gift of the Koran to humanity. During the fast which goes on for an entire lunar month, a Muslim entirely abstains from eating or drinking from dawn to dusk. No smokes either. After sundown, every day a celebratory feast is held. Before dawn, people load up for the long hungry day ahead. The purpose of fasting is to cleanse the spirit, teach self-discipline, and remind believers of what it feels like to go without. Pregnant women, nursing mothers, children under ten, soldiers at war, and travellers are not obliged to fast during Ramadan.

The timing of Ramadan follows the lunar calendar, so the exact day of its advent is not known until one or two days beforehand. That was why the gaol religious authorities were in such a twitter of anticipation. The lunar month is shorter than the month of the Gregorian calendar, and Muslim festivals move forward eleven days per Western calendar year. Therefore the season in which Ramadan falls changes over time.

While we were in Ruwais prison, Ramadan fell at the hottest time of the year; late July. It must be terribly difficult to go without even a teaspoon of drink when the temperature is 45 degrees or more. Nevertheless, most of the prisoners seemed to scrupulously follow the edicts of their faith.

The end of Ramadan is marked by a celebration called Eid al Fitr.

For prisoners, that is also a time when amnesties are awarded. Of an evening during Ramadan, we dined in great style on roast lamb, rice, sardines in oil, Arab bread and jam. After the all-day fast, it was a true feast. My most succulent memory of that long month is of the jam. Before Ramadan, I had longed for it.

Four of us – Tim Hayter, Dieter Chapuis, Manfred Schlaefer and I – were half-heartedly playing poker the day before. I think jackpots with the short pack is a much better game than straight full-pack poker, but there is less bluffing.

◨◪◨

TUESDAY 24 JULY
Total poker losses 680 riyals.
Arranged to visit Kit Wilkinson, the dentist at Bakhsh Hospital.
When I arrived, Kit was treating Agnes Johnstone, the hospital matron.

'Richard, I sent over some copies of the *British Medical Journal* to you last night,' Agnes told me. I had not received them. That was hardly surprising as items sent to me often went missing.

Kit fixed both teeth. Agnes produced some Tang and made up a cool drink for us. Kit uncommunicative but I gathered he was disillusioned with hospital. Said Bakhsh was losing control. Still only sixty beds open.

I collected some photographs of the children from my office for Penny and also tried on a *thobe* I found. It fitted me well and I decided to wear it in the prison for comfort.

After Kit had finished with me, I went to see Dr Bakhsh, whom I had not seen or heard from for a while. He was extremely friendly to me, which, given our previous history, I found surprising.

'I am sorry I did not come to visit you in gaol,' he told me. 'Last time, the guard at the gate did not want to let me out and so I was afraid to come again.'

'If you telephone Captain Saad in advance,' I tried to assure the friendly Dr Bakhsh, 'there will be no problem.'

'Ah, I see.'

He paused. 'And I will try to find out about your case from the Governor of Mecca's office before I see you again.'

'Thank you.'

Was fully searched by Ali when I got back; I think Saad thought I might bring a camera or something back in and tipped him off.

◫◲◫

WEDNESDAY 25 JULY

Wedding anniversary.

I got someone in prison to sketch the children from photographs as an anniversary present for Penny.

Heard a horror story from a young Pakistani prisoner: a motor-cyclist rode into rear of his car and was killed. The Pakistani got six months in prison and has to pay the family 42 000 riyals.

A guard took me to Saad's office. After a long wait, they got Penny. We had about an hour and a half chat with Tang and biscuits, first in Saad's office, and then in another one, smelling of cat shit, across the passage. Gave Penny the two pencil prints of the children which she liked.

◫◲◫

SUNDAY 29 JULY

Had a surprise visit from Pip Reddaway and Sharon Parmenter of the Australian community. They told me that Alan, who has been on leave, has decided not to return to Saudi Arabia. A wise move, I thought.

Alan was the doctor from whom we bought the whisky for our party. As doctor with one of the large companies, he had lived with other employees in a huge compound. You can do pretty well what you like in them and he had developed a little sideline – supplying alcohol to people outside the compound. I think he is afraid that somebody may have dobbed him in for supplying us with whisky for the party.

As well as Pip and Sharon, my other most frequent and loyal visitors are two British women, Angela de Klee and Judy Hindle. Between them all, they organised a visiting roster, the outcome being that the stretch between Thursdays seemed to shrink.

I owe the four women a great debt.

◰◱◲

FRIDAY 27 JULY

Ahmed spitting out his saliva like a good boy. During Ramadan, believers are not even supposed to swallow their own saliva and so they are all spitting which is revolting.

Graham Piper, the transport contractor I met here in Ruwais, has decided not to try to come back to work here any more. He will take his trucks empty back to UK. He has offered to take our car plus all our belongings back to UK in one of his trucks. Isn't that nice of him?

◰◱◲

SATURDAY 28 JULY

Collared by Abdul Salam, ex-pilot, ex-banker, just completing ten years for importing 4 kg raw opium, to see his dead fish. He has six super aquariums of fresh fish, one of which has fish dying of a fungal infection. Suggested he talk to Jacques, who is a marine biologist as well as a diver and also try doubling up on a dose of anti-fungal treatment.

Occasionally, during these months in prison, the dreaded desert wind, the khamsin, blows. One afternoon, the temperature soared to 45 degrees for an hour or two. The wind howled and everything was soon covered with a film of fine red dust. That night there was another terrific dust storm, with thunder and lightning. It was slightly cooler the following day but no rain.

SUNDAY 29 JULY
Only one fish has died in the past 24 hours.

I was invited by Captain Saad to his office. Over cups of tea, we talked in a relaxed manner. I was too relaxed; once or twice I inadvertently let slip pieces of information that I should have kept to myself.

'What are the people like in your section?' he asked.

'Oh, they seem to get on well,' I laughed, 'there's a lot of kissing and hugging among some of them and a few double ender trips to the loo.'

I told him of those who went off, two by two, to the end cubicle. 'And Ali seems to have a penchant for little boys.'

As soon as I said this, I could have bitten my tongue. But it was too late. Captain Saad went straight to the section and Ali, who was then in charge of my room, received twenty-five lashes on the soles of his feet as punishment.

I felt a bit of a shit when I went back to the cell later that day. A very subdued Ali huddled in the corner. But the others thought it was a fine joke and Ali was soon grinning away with the rest of them. To my surprise, I found myself lionised by everyone over this incident.

Ali's two-year sentence was almost up, too. With only one month more to go, he told me about his increasing anxiety and nervousness. He had become tense and aggressive. (Another reason why I should not have dobbed him in.)

His apprehension at impending change seemed understandable. There were frustrations certainly in prison but no real worries as such, unless you were facing a death sentence. We were fed, we slept, we occupied the time as best we could. In the outside world, one has to think and do things and make a living, make plans. I observed what these men were going through and empathised. 'Such nervousness at the end of the time a person is in gaol is typical,' Captain Saad told me.

MONDAY 30 JULY

Spoke to a new prisoner called Charles Fussell last night. Motor vehicle accident two months ago — child killed.

Blood money paid by his company.

It has been quite a strain at times living with these Arabs. The continuing shifts of allegiances and friendships were quite wearing and, as Gonfidi and Abdullah's lover, Yeh Yeh, talk until 3.30 or later and then resume chattering at 5.00 or 6.00, it does not make for easy sleeping. God knows how they manage as they don't sleep all that much during the day.

Yeh Yeh has 'gaol fever', too. Unable to sleep at night, he is constantly tired, snoozing at intervals during the day, but also feeling over-alert, over-stimulated. Yeh Yeh complained to me of feeling unwell so I wrote a note for him to give to Dr Abbas at the prison clinic, suggesting he be given 100 milligrams of Largactil daily to calm him down.

Toilets pretty disgraceful at the moment; quarter have doors missing. Another blocked, with shit all over the place. Broom without handle in corner not effective.

Reading book on ESP. Tried to communicate with Penny by ESP at 12 noon and 12 midnight. Thinking of a red rose, full house poker hand — 3s x 2, Queens x 3.

◰◱◲

TUESDAY 31 JULY

Klaus now gets to cook food during the day for the gawajas, because it is still Ramadan.

Toothache terrible this morning. Two Panadol did the trick for six hours. Got to Bakhsh Hospital with difficulty about 12 — place deserted.

Noticed all balcony rails in flats raised by about 15 to 20 cm. New rails still unpainted.

Very hot. Wrote letters.

Toothache settled down eventually. The amaliad had sleeping guards all over it, including the desk.

◫◳◫

WEDNESDAY 1 AUGUST
Penny and children to England.

I had written this in black at the top of the page. We had intended that Penny and the children would go back for a holiday at this time before this all happened and I had noted it in the diary.

Toothache terrible again. Went to see Captain Saad. Got permission to go to Kit Wilkinson this evening without caleshe (handcuffs). Tried to see Penny but not allowed.

Had an excellent afternoon of poker, winning 200 riyals (offset debts of 700 riyals) and no toothache at all until after supper – then terrible again.

Went to amaliad and little guard very unhappy about no caleshe. We intercepted Suleiman, the chief of the prison, after prayers and he said it was OK.

Kit took tooth out with difficulty. It looked pretty manky. The problem was probably a crack which allowed matter to trickle down. Hellish painful after the local anaesthetic wore off despite three Panadol.

◫◳◫

THURSDAY 2 AUGUST
Got some sleep as the pain gradually eased.

Got to see Penny with not much difficulty at about 1 p.m. as I was sure she wanted to see me. This was the ESP again. Bulldozed my way out ahead of guard who came with me to the amaliad. There were three guards asleep there, one completely shrouded and on the desk.

They were too sleepy to argue, so we let ourselves out of the main gate. The rifle guard there had vanished and we walked to the women's section. Penny was fetched in a few minutes and we chatted for about twenty minutes.

She is worried that Francis Geere and others, as well as the Saudi authorities think there really was an orgy with drink, sex and drugs. We must make sure they understand this is not so.

After I got back to my own section, and was held up in the office, about twenty people came in wearing thick *thobes* for their beatings. But they had to strip off the many layers of clothes they were wearing.

Also thirty bods from our section had five lashes apiece on the feet for breaking the Ramadan fast.

These were my hardest days in prison. I was physically unwell, suffering from what seemed to be a succession of ailments. I started to lose hope. Ill health was a constant source of anxiety among the prisoners. Even the most trivial health problems seemed to be magnified in gaol.

I felt constant pain and discomfort. Nothing seemed to be happening with our case. I was stuck here, in this hell. This was my low point. I missed England: the smell of the London pavement after a hard night's rain, the sound of the wind rushing and howling through the trees, the sight of white snowdrops pushing their way through bleak black soil after a long arduous winter.

I longed for cosy evenings by a roaring log fire, long country walks, shuffling through clumps of crisp autumn leaves and I longed for snow — vast quantities of white enchantment.

I missed the scent of freshly mown grass, the glint of sunlight through wooden fence slats, and the sweet taste of strawberry jam, and above all, I prayed for the sight of just one cumulus cloud to break the endless monotony of the brazen blue skies.

I craved the gentle relaxed conversation and polite reserve of the British. I wished for the company of loving friends.

I wanted freedom.

I was Dr Gawaja, prisoner in Saudi Arabia, incarcerated, and surrounded by assorted thieves, villains and even murderers.

Get me out of here!

That night was the closest that I came to regret.

◨◧◨

After weeks of delay, we were informed that Francis Geere and the German consul are to go to Taif to speak on our behalf to the Ministry of the Interior. I made two requests to Francis; first that he discover, once and for all, whether the police had completed their investigations into the deaths, and second, whether we could expect any surprises in the Ramadan amnesty.

It was customary for the Governor of Mecca to release chosen prisoners as a gesture of kindness at the end of the month-long fast. This seemed, however, a vain hope for us; no foreign prisoners had ever been released under the Ramadan amnesty.

◨◧◨

SATURDAY 4 AUGUST
I was summoned early to Captain Saad's office.

'I have received a telex from the Governor of Mecca's office,' he announced, smiling. 'He has agreed to Penelope's release under guarantee.'

It was the best news we had received in almost three months. I was allowed to go and break the news to Penny. Later, when we returned together to Saad's office, Angela de Klee was waiting there. 'Yes, the telex is true,' she said.

'So when can Penny leave?'

—134—

'It's not quite as simple as that. Francis Geere tells me it is not possible for her to stay with us at the embassy.' That was where she and her husband, the military attaché, lived.

Never-ending setbacks; I gave Angela the number of an Arab businessman I knew. Perhaps he could sponsor Penny.

Our troubles seemed far from over.

'You will need letters from the relatives of Helen and Johannes before you can finally be set free,' a prisoner told me.

'Why?'

'The relatives need to write that they release you from any guilt in the deaths.'

'I've never heard of that. Are you sure?'

'I am certain.'

Unconvinced, I decided that Penny could get to the bottom of that problem after she was out. If it should indeed be the case, she could arrange for someone to visit Helen's family in England and Harms Salvage could telex Germany to get them to organise the same with Johannes' family.

The very next day, Penny was released. Or so I thought. Late in the day, I was called to Captain Saad's office to find her there in a state of despondency.

'We've been driving around Jeddah in a truck for over four hours,' she told me. 'We visited five police stations but none of them could give me the release for my guarantee.'

Penny spent the night back in prison. The following day she was taken to the Sharifia police station where the necessary formalities were completed.

However, there was still the problem of the release under guarantee. Gordon Kirby of the British Embassy informed us the guarantee had to be given by my sponsor, in this case, Dr Bakhsh. He eventually agreed, but on condition that the British Embassy was responsible for Penny. The two documents had then to be approved by the Saudi authorities before she could be let out.

Two more days went by.

Finally, all the papers were in order. And permission had been granted for Penny to stay with the de Klees at the British Embassy.

◧◖◧

WEDNESDAY 8 AUGUST
Penny barra.

Barra means 'outside'. That was the great cry that went up when a prisoner was let out.

'I'm sad to be leaving you, Richard.'

'Don't worry, I'll be fine.'

We said our goodbyes in the office, in front of Gordon Kirby and Dr Bakhsh. The latter looked stern.

'You are not to go to the hospital,' he told Penny.

'We have heard from Ron Smith,' Gordon Kirby told me. 'Apparently he is on his way back to Saudi Arabia with a large dossier on Helen's supposed murder. He is due this evening.'

None of us, except Penny, seemed unduly worried.

'There was no murder. What information can he possibly have?' I fumed. 'He can't possibly do anything to us.'

Penny did not look so confident.

◧◖◧

I was becoming accustomed to my life in prison. I even looked forward to pay day. Everyone received fifty-two riyals a week to buy things. It was not much, only enough to buy a few Pepsis or some fruit.

I was now embroiled in daily events and the inner politics of the block. Karim (the young man who had fibbed to Martin about being in for murder) was due to leave for another prison, and there was a big fuss in the cell. Who would buy his mattress and who would take over his corner spot? Karim tried to sell me his mattress for 400 riyals. I was not interested. He dropped the price to 150 but I still declined.

By rights of seniority, the corner spot should go to Ahmed, who was serving a couple of years for allegedly molesting a girl.

I felt I was part of the group finally when Mohammed Masri, the gentlemanly Egyptian school teacher, in an effort to insult me (I forget why), called me a kaffir. This is the derogatory Arabic term for a non-Muslim, an unbeliever. It is also the insult used for blacks in South Africa. I found it ironic that I, a white person, should be called a kaffir by a dark-skinned person.

回단回

FRIDAY 17 AUGUST
Got to bed about 6 a.m. and at 7 the fans stopped, until about 11. It was terribly hot and we were all drenched with sweat within a few minutes.

Harms lunch hamper arrived as expected 4 p.m. Martin, Harry, Tim and Dieter fell on it like wolves. I was also very hungry but when I moved across and asked if there was any for me, Harry said shortly, 'No, I don't think so'. Rude bastard. Don't know what is going on.

回단回

SATURDAY 18 AUGUST
The start of the Ramadan amnesty. Many extra guards were brought in. A committee will sit for the next five days to decide who will be let go. As far as we know, no unbelieving gawajas have ever been released under the amnesty. But we did not expect to be included anyway.

回단回

FRIDAY 7 SEPTEMBER
Johnson's Prickly Heat soap brought by Penny on her visit the other day is most effective.

I occupied myself making notes about what I would say to Dr Bakhsh when I next saw him. I had to ask him for my back salary for a start. I gave up a good career in the United Kingdom to come out here. I had worked hard for him and had developed personal contacts with other general practitioners in Jeddah and the large Western companies. I really felt Dr Bakhsh owed me for the discomfort I had been through in the past months in prison. The accident had not been my fault. If anything, the hospital was partly to blame. On several occasions, Penny and I had complained about the low balcony rails. I did not wish his hospital harm but I could sue him in the United Kingdom for wages.

ロ凸ロ

SUNDAY 9 SEPTEMBER
Asked for a note from the British Embassy to say Penny and I are married so we can have a 'special visit'.

Captain Saad informed me that the police had found Johannes Otten's passport, which took me aback. We had found it ourselves, on that first day, 20 May. Another bizarre note was struck when I was told that our case had gone beyond the Governor of Mecca and was now before the Saudi Cabinet. They would ask the courts to come to a rapid decision about us. It all sounded back to front to me.

On 14 September someone from the British Embassy told me the Governor of Mecca would discuss the case with a cabinet committee. 'It is not a full cabinet matter'. I thought this showed just how confused everyone was about us. I worried that it would limp on for ages. Keith Hindle, Judy's husband, has asked a lawyer friend of his, Mujahid al Sawaaf, to look into our case. News comes through that the German Ambassador has visited the Governor of Mecca.

Finally Francis Geere brought with him to the prison Stanley Duncan, head of the communication section of the Foreign Office. A straightforward man, he was slightly apologetic, and admitted he could not do much to help. But he assured me London was very busy on our behalf. 'Your case is going to a Council of Ministers who will try to expedite matters.'

A local Arab doctor promised Penny he would see the King and the Governor of Mecca on our behalf. Fine promises but nothing came of them.

Our new Saudi lawyer, Mujahid al Sawaaf, made an appointment to speak with the Minister of Justice this week.

The most down-to-earth suggestion comes from the British *chargé d'affaires*. He tells Penny of one fellow who, after waiting patiently for an entire year at the embassy just upped and took off. Perhaps we should try this ourselves.

回凸回

SATURDAY 22 SEPTEMBER
Woken at 8 by Abdul Aziz for breakfast — beans, hot milk, jam and bread. I went to the library about 8.30. Reading 'Arterial Surgery' and going well.

I had a scientific paper published in an international medical journal, concerning some research work I had carried out in London the previous year. It amused me that I was in prison at the time of publication, a first for a doctor I would have thought.

Klaus Ritter again almost succumbed to heatstroke today, and I learned Peter de Cito finally died of cancer of the larynx.

回凸回

MONDAY 24 SEPTEMBER
I have begun to find the prison food quite nauseating. I nearly puked today while trying to eat some boiled chicken and rice. It was a real effort to get it down. The rest of the diet I also find quite horrid — boiled beef and beans. The breakfast is not bad but it comes at 7.30 which is often only an hour or two after I have got to sleep. So that is not much good.

Fortunately the Harms Salvage food supplies continue, and I am again allowed to share, and they are a help.

Ibrahim Gonfidi has opened a 'shop' which sells biscuits. They keep me going.

Surprise change; women visiting this morning between 9 a.m. and 1 p.m. I tried to phone Penny, tried bribing a guard to phone her, but no senior officers here today and permission refused. Sod it. Slept heavily, 10 till 1, in disgust.

On 26 September the Germans had a visit from their Ambassador. The German Embassy has been galvanised into action by a telex from Bonn. At last there was hope for some action, I thought.

The weather is definitely cooling off a bit but my room seems much hotter than the rest and I am still sweating like a pig. The prickly heat reached an all-time high and my neck and chest became severely affected. I think this was aggravated by 'flannel trauma' as I have been washing very vigorously. I shifted back to hand washing and, with a combined attack of Prickly Heat soap and special powder, it seemed to be settling. Some of the Arabs had prickly heat really badly and it developed into a generalised infected rash with tiny pustules. Two chaps had severe impetigo, one on his arms and chest and the other on his scalp, with several large carbuncles on his shoulder.

回리回

MONDAY 1 OCTOBER
Life in the room is nice and peaceful. I laid down the law today regarding 'extras', including Gonfidi's 'whore'. The section is so crowded – 196 bods.

Spoke to Hassan who is trying to get several people shifted to other sections.

I was getting quite cocky at this stage, a real veteran.
Each room has a boss who is in charge of behaviour in that room

and also has to keep it clean and tidy if he wants to avoid a beating from the guards. By now, I am the third senior person in the room.

◧◨◧

WEDNESDAY 3 OCTOBER

Very hot at the moment. Not going to the clinic any more. About 80 per cent of the patients there have nothing seriously wrong with them, just want to have a walk out of their sections and get some pills.

Told off Martin Fleischer for letting himself be seen giving Tim Hayter an Aspro. Any sort of pill here is regarded as a drug, even an aspirin.

As August became September and moved on into October, the Germans and I decided it was most unlikely that we would be out before the end of the year, so we started to make plans for Christmas.

◧◨◧

FRIDAY 5 OCTOBER

Woken at 7.30 by Mohammed for breakfast, then slept till 10.30. Good wash with ice water which Mohammed got for me. Wrote letter to Mother. Snoozing at 5 when called out to see Captain Saad. He took me into his office and asked me about a little girl with bilateral webbed toes (I think it was his daughter). I told him to wait until she is five or six and have them separated.

Saad phoned the embassy for me and I spoke to Penny for some time. She had tried to come in Tuesday, Wednesday and Thursday but had been turned back at the gate.

◧◨◧

SATURDAY 6 OCTOBER

Reason why gaol is so tight at the moment is that somebody escaped from section two days ago – just walked out.

TUESDAY 9 OCTOBER

Given 'Pearl' by Maurice. High-grade Victorian porno book. Hassan, the Egyptian baker, very low today as he has just been told his sister died in Cairo, aged 18. Gave him some aspirin. And then gave him 'Pearl' to cheer him up.

FRIDAY 12 OCTOBER

One young Yemeni took a one-way trip to the market place this morning. He had waited here for three years under death sentence. Taken in the morning with two other Yemenis (non-capital) who were then sent back.

He was handcuffed, chained and taken away. Executed at 1.20 p.m.

SATURDAY 13 OCTOBER

Surprise visit from Angela de Klee and Judy Hindle. Angela explained political activity our case has stirred up. Apparently we caused such a furore among the faithful they want to chastise all Westerners.

Our lawyer, Mujahid al Sawaaf, later confirms this and thinks we have a chance now that the dust has settled. He is visiting the Ministry of Justice again on our behalf.

SUNDAY 14 OCTOBER

11 a.m. Special visit.

Had a leisurely breakfast. Given 'colonia'. [This is a liberal dousing in perfume. My Arab fellow-prisoners are crazy about it.] *Called to Captain Saad's office at 10.55. Penny furious at having to wait in Saad's office. She felt everybody was watching her. They probably were. Special visit room bare but for a mattress and filthy walls, cracked plaster.*

We had a lovely time for five hours.

Got dressed at 2, expecting to be called but weren't, so lay and chatted some more and were called at 4 at a most inopportune moment.

Nice lunch provided by Judy.

回己回

MONDAY 15 OCTOBER
Felt very tired all day.

Chatted to an Australian nicknamed the 'Jeddah Axeman'. Hit a Brit on the head with a hammer. Here now for three years, Taif for six months. He seems very sane and healthy now and is on reducing doses of Largactil. He gave me 50 mg which I took this evening and had a great sleep.

回己回

TUESDAY 16 OCTOBER
Slight hangover from Largactil.

At last, real news came about our case. Dr al Sawaaf met with the Deputy Minister of the Interior. He told al Sawaaf that our papers have gone to Prince Fawaz (Governor of Mecca) for him to decide on either a court case or maybe deportation. We will hear as early as the following day.

Early morning of 17 October, I was called to Captain Saad's office where, to my great surprise and delight, Penny is sitting. She has a grin from ear to ear. 'Great news! A telegram is being sent from the Saudi Minister of the Interior, Prince Naif, to the Governor of Mecca's office recommending that Arnot's case be closed. Dr Arnot to be released. Can you believe it?'

No, I couldn't. There was still no word about deportation or about the Germans. Nevertheless, on my return to the cell, I told everyone. Jacques Texier was fairly philosophical about the whole matter. Harry Goodside, Harms Salvage boss, was his usual querulous self. Then the Germans were all called out to have their names checked at the *amaliad*. So something must be happening.

◻|🔁|◻

WEDNESDAY 24 OCTOBER
157 days since I was arrested.

I was taken to the *amaliad* to find my release papers there. My *batarga* (prison identity document) number was duly recorded and I was sent back to the prison to pack. To pack? What did I have? It took me all of ten minutes to reappear, ready for my release.

'No, you're not out yet, maybe Saturday.'

'How can this be? Let me see Captain Saad.'

Saad confirmed the Saturday release date.

So, dejected and deflated, I returned to the section.

At 2.30 that afternoon, all our names were called out on the tannoy and we went out, expecting just to have our *batarga* numbers recorded. Suddenly the guards started shackling us together. We were to be released after all.

'If we're to be released, let us take our things,' we pleaded.

We were marched out, two by two, to be taken to the Sharifia for the final documents to be signed. Then, there turned out to be no transport. Our freedom was to be delayed for lack of a vehicle.

'Can't you get one from somewhere?'

No. It seemed we were to be taken back to our cells. Then one of the Germans had a great idea.

'We'll get taxis.' The guards looked dubious.

'We'll pay for them and we'll pay for the guards to come back to the prison.' After some reluctance, the guards agreed. And then the bus arrived after all.

The lieutenant at the Sharifia was snoozing, with his shoes off. Surprised to see us, and at first reluctant, he finally agreed to release all of us, but only after the papers had been signed by the Saudi sponsor. This was fast becoming a farce. But we were determined not to lose our chance of release.

The Germans quickly tried to contact their sponsor and I rang Penny who told me Dr Bakhsh and Francis Geere would arrive at six o'clock that evening. Jacques was in a spot as he had no Saudi sponsor.

We waited impatiently in the yard of the Sharifia, where all this had started in May. The sponsor of the Germans could not be found. Dr Bakhsh's driver arrived with a letter and Francis Geere came at 6.45. Dr Bakhsh's letter was deemed inadequate and so the driver was sent off to get another one which was 'better'. Mission accomplished, papers were approved and signed and I was on my way, the driver dragging me out as if a bomb was about to go off.

The Germans and Jacques Texier were left at the Sharifia. Their sponsor refused to guarantee them, having been caught once before by people jumping bond. Their problem was, however, sorted out and the rest of our group, including Tim, were soon out of prison.

I reached the de Klees' residence at the British Embassy at 8.00 p.m. and had a cool drink in my hand by 8.05. Marvellous.

Open arrest, Jeddah

A photograph of myself, newly released from prison, shows a lean and gaunt face staring back at the camera. The eyes look directly ahead, betraying no emotion. The expression gives nothing away.

It felt strange to be free at last. Sleeping in a real bed with proper bed linen, rather than on a thin rubber mat, gave me an extraordinary sensation of luxury. I felt privileged to be able to wear fresh, clean clothes and to eat decent food.

For the first couple of nights, I used to wake up and wonder what I was doing out of prison. Despite the slight feeling of unreality, I can't recall having any nightmares though.

I was shocked when I looked in the mirror and saw how much weight I had lost, almost ten kilos. The following morning showed me how physically weak I had become; I could barely swim a length of the embassy pool without puffing. Weeks of sitting around in the gaol with no exercise had taken their toll. Now, even a short walk quickly tired me.

The embassy compound in Jeddah is on the eastern side of the city. The area is surrounded by a high wall and covers about 200 hectares. Armed guards are permanently stationed at each gate. In the compound, staff live in apartments or houses, depending on their status. Inside the compound walls, they are free to do virtually anything they like.

The British Embassy was one of the first to be constructed. The prohibition on foreigners and non-Muslims having alcohol in Saudi Arabia came about because of an incident that took place at the British Embassy in Jeddah, in 1951.

The British consul had lived in Saudi Arabia for twenty years. He regularly entertained Saudi friends, and served alcohol which in those days foreigners were permitted to import. A young prince, by the name of Mishari Abdul Aziz, a son of the king, became drunk at one of the consul's parties, and started a row.

The prince went home, got a rifle, and returned to the consul's house. He began to shoot up the place. The British consul was shot dead as he tried to help his wife escape the bullets. He is buried in Jeddah cemetery.

Prince Mishari was imprisoned, but not executed. Heartbroken, King Abdul Aziz banned alcohol from the entire kingdom. The ban was in force when Penny and I lived in Jeddah, and still applies at the time of writing.

◧⌘◨

My overwhelming feeling during those first days of freedom was of pleasure rather than relief. I took delight in anything and everything – coming and going as I pleased, driving through the streets, watching the crowds of people, and even the traffic.

We stayed for a while with Colonel Murray de Klee, the British military attaché, and his wife Angela. We had known them from London and we were grateful for their kindness while we were in prison, and their present hospitality. Unfortunately, some of the embassy staff seemed to regard us as virtual criminals whereas we considered ourselves to be the innocent victims of circumstances. We were often reminded that we were a nuisance.

Quite soon, Sir John Onslow and his wife Sue, whom we met at an embassy party, took us under their wing. Sir John was captain of King Khalid's yacht, the Saudi Arabian equivalent of the RY *Britannia*, and when they heard of the problems we were facing at the embassy, they invited us to live in the spare house in their compound.

John and Sue became great friends of ours, and helped us to recover from the experiences of months past. Because Sue came from

Melbourne, they introduced us to a great number of the Australians living in Jeddah. We started to build up a new social circle.

Penny and I often joined the friendly throng at the so-called Dead Dingo in the Australian Embassy.

'Strange name,' I commented once.

'There's nothing in the world as dry as a dead dingo's donger, Richard,' explained one of the embassy staff, 'and by the end of the week we are dry.'

We bumped into Tim Hayter there once or twice. I was not interested in talking to him. I felt embittered about what had happened between him and Penny. His presence made me feel angry and reminded me of my poor marriage, and that it was too painful and unpleasant to study closely.

Penny was offered a part-time job as a secretary at the Australian Embassy. The income she brought in was extremely useful as I was no longer allowed to work, due to all the notoriety surrounding our case. Dr Bakhsh had refused my request to resume work at the hospital. I had to occupy my time with the other activities that Jeddah had to offer.

My strength returned quite rapidly and I built up my fitness with a healthy diet and adequate exercise – swimming and walking.

Despite its punitive aspect, house arrest seemed like a vacation. It gave me a chance to unwind and to begin to recover from the horrors of the previous months. Forbidden to work, I took up scuba diving, usually with Jacques Texier. I visited Jacques on his boat, the caique moored at Obhor Creek. Although somewhat battered, to me it was a lovely vessel, and I was anxious to make the most of the area's superb diving spots.

'That black coral is beautiful,' I commented to Jacques on one visit as he proudly showed me his spoils.

'Take it, please,' he said, handing over the superb specimen. 'We can dive together and collect some more if you like.'

There were numerous outcrops of the semi-precious black coral in the Obhor Creek. There were plans to drain the creek, and so

I determined to salvage specimens, if I could. On one spectacular dive, I came across an enormous tree of black coral, over two metres high. I cut off a branch and took it ashore with difficulty. Later, I built a frame around it and crated it back to England by sea. I presented it to the British Museum.

One morning, on the south side of the Obhor Creek, not far from its mouth, I found myself in a virtual forest of black coral. The many offcuts lying on the sandy ground were evidence of recent visitors. I, too, helped myself to pieces of the hard material, and sold them later to a jeweller for 2700 riyals.

Penny sometimes joined me in the dives. We swam gently along the reefs, among the spectacular coral and multicoloured fish of the Red Sea.

At weekends, our friends Terry and Linda Bennett took us out on their fifteen-metre New England fishing boat to spots where the water was so clear we were obliged to wear T-shirts to avoid getting sunburnt, even under water. Terry and Linda had lived in Jeddah for five years and, quite uniquely for a non-Arab, Terry not merely survived, but prospered in general practice.

One of our favourite offshore reefs was Wreck Reef, named for the remains of a boat easily visible forty metres below. We swam down to the wreck and explored its nooks and crannies, which had attracted a great population of reef fish over the years. We saw numerous barracuda and harmless reef sharks which Terry hunted with a powerful spear gun that used .22 calibre blank cartridges.

At Wreck Reef, I collected several long, pointy, pale-coloured shells known as augers. On another dive, we spotted several sharks while we were swimming down to explore a sunken dhow and a small freighter. On another dive, my diving 'buddy', who had speared some fish and attached them to his weight belt, had his catch snatched off by a large shark that happened to be passing. In doing so, it gave him a violent nudge, but did not leave a mark on him.

As well as exploring Obhor Creek, we used to drive along the coast from Jeddah, both north or south, to shore reefs where we camped on the beach and lived off whatever fish we speared. One memorable trip included a number of diplomats from the Australian Embassy, including the Australian Ambassador to Saudi Arabia. Another fascinating dive we made was at night, with one of the British Embassy signallers, during which he showed us hundreds of shellfish reflected in the light from our torches.

◧◿◨

Horse riding in the desert, despite the lack of vegetation, reminded of my childhood days in the Transvaal. That had been on a maize and cattle farm near Johannesburg. The place was also a guest farm and had dozens of riding horses. There, we children were taught to ride as if we had been born to it. I was more keen on horses than my brothers. I used to go out early each morning, barefoot in the dewy grass and catch my horse, enticing him with grain from my pocket. I slipped a bridle over his head there in the veldt and led him to a rock or anthill so as I could scramble on to his back. Bareback, I then rounded up the rest of the working horses and brought them into the yard for the day's riding.

There was not much wet grass around Jeddah. But it was open riding and I felt as free as I had in my childhood. Even though there were several thousand square kilometres of desert I could have ridden away into, it was still very much a cage. I was a prisoner, but able to ride out into the desert and maybe disappear completely if I chose. I decided against it.

The stables of Jeddah were in the desert just outside town. They housed a number of pure bred Arab racehorses. Local racing practice did not include much training as the Saudis followed the traditional Bedouin method of racing their horses 'cold'. In earlier times, the horses would have been constantly exercised in the course of their day-to-day work. But the Toyota and Land Rover had taken the place of horses and camels. Horses now stood in their stables for months on end, eating high-energy feed, occasionally being taken to the track and raced flat out.

Many of the horses broke down under this sort of treatment and I was asked to ride one such Arab ex-racer. A three-year-old mare with a placid nature, she had just two gaits – a slow walk or a flat-out gallop. Her gallop was incredibly exciting. She went until she dropped with exhaustion. The only way I could make her stop was to guide her towards a high sand dune and keep her at it, until she could go no further up the soft sloping sand. There she would finally halt, flanks heaving, gasping for breath and I would gaze out across the vast endless desert expanses.

These expeditions gave us an illusion of freedom and, for a while, Penny and I were able to forget that we were prisoners of the Saudis, and still separated from our two little children.

Penny and I were on our own, left to sort out our own situation. Our relationship at that time was tolerable but not the best. We talked a lot, but not about the party or our predicament. Penny made it plain that she was pretty sick of our marriage and really wanted it to end. I was desperately trying not to let that happen, so as not to lose the children. That was my greatest fear. It was clear enough that Penny and I were incompatible but I was prepared to carry on. As things turned out, I lost the children anyway.

◻◻◻

The Saudi Arabian lawyer, Dr Mujahid al Sawaaf, whom we had engaged shortly before I left prison, had an open, efficient and cheerful manner and spoke excellent English. I took an instant liking to him. He was extremely reassuring and I felt confident in his ability. He was, of course, thoroughly acquainted with the Saudi judicial system.

Dr al Sawaaf's first piece of advice to Penny and Tim was that their statements, if true, were bound to get them into terrible trouble. 'Both of you face possible execution,' he explained to Penny, 'as you have both admitted to adultery.'

On my own problem of Dr Bakhsh refusing my request to resume work at the hospital, Dr al Sawaaf advised, 'You must find out on what grounds Dr Bakhsh will not let you work. Ask him whether he intends to terminate your contract.'

'I don't know how he can do that,' I said. 'I am on salary. He has no right to stop me working.'

'Please keep it friendly,' al Sawaaf insisted, sensing my frustration and anger.

Later that week, I managed to keep my temper as the apparently muddled Dr Bakhsh told me he intended to end my contract as from the previous 20 May. He then informed me, rather mystifyingly, he would have to consult his own lawyer as to the reason he would give.

Four days later, I received the bad news.

'Penny, I can't believe this. Dr Bakhsh's lawyer says I am unfit to practise medicine and that Dr Bakhsh has every right not to employ me. And what's more, he says Dr Bakhsh does not need to pay me after 20 May of this year.'

'Calm down, Richard,' Penny tried to reassure me. But her attempts were futile. I felt shocked and humiliated. And I was scared. I had no future in Saudi Arabia, and I had no income. What was to become of us?

Dr al Sawaaf was more philosophical about my situation.

'Now we know where we stand,' was his response.

'But this is a very nasty, very harsh opinion,' I told al Sawaaf.

'Perhaps,' he smiled, 'but now we know where we stand,' he repeated.

I was finding it difficult to be so relaxed. My own view was much more gloomy.

My spirits lifted for a while that evening when Penny insisted we visit our friends, the Hindles, where we watched a video of *Midnight Express*. That story of an American drug smuggler's incarceration in a Turkish prison and eventual escape would never have been screened publicly in Saudi Arabia.

Our good mood was short lived. The following day, 20 November 1979, was a black day.

'Have you heard?'

'No. What's happened?'

'Some dissident Saudi tribesmen attacked the mosque in Mecca this morning. A lot of people have been killed. You will be affected,' Dr al Sawaaf informed us glumly. 'Public feeling is that the government has been too soft on foreigners.'

Dr al Sawaaf was right again. Shortly after the end of the Hajj annual pilgrimage, at dawn, that day, 20 November, a group of Saudi religious zealots took over the Grand Mosque at Mecca. The Grand Mosque is the Islamic holy of holies, with direct links all the way back to Mohammed, then to the ancient patriarch, Abraham, and even further again.

The extremists were protesting against the degeneration of Islam in the modern world, as well as what they perceived to be the moral corruption of the Saudi royal family. Among their number, the religious group had also discovered a young man whom they nominated as the Mahdi, or messiah.

For a week, the zealots fought off the Saudi armed forces sent in to tear-gas and shoot them out of the Grand Mosque. By the time the bloody little campaign was over, more than 200 people had been killed; rebels and Saudi army personnel, as well as worshippers.

The Saud family were embarrassed, as much by their apparent inability to look after the holy places of Islam, as by the accusations of greed and moral laxity levelled at them by the rebels. The mere presence of so many foreigners on the Arab peninsula offended the prejudices of religious extremists. And this is where Penny and I came in; we were foreign, accused of breaking Saudi law, but yet to be sentenced.

A Flogging after Christmas

Christmas 1979 was pretty dismal.

Non-Muslim religious buildings and services are entirely prohibited on the Arabian peninsula, so even Christmas must be celebrated underhand, and unofficially. A Church of England minister came especially from somewhere like Cyprus that year. There was a service of sorts at the British Embassy, in a makeshift area in one of the small reception rooms.

We may have gone to a Christmas party, I really can't recall. My only memory is of an unpleasant atmosphere during the traditional season of goodwill, still trapped in an alien country.

Christmas. A time to reflect. A time to ponder. Had I been too impetuous, too reckless? Were rash decisions, such as coming to Saudi Arabia, my downfall? Did I have only myself to blame? Or would my punishment in Saudi Arabia leave me with some long-lasting benefits?

New Year turned out worse than Christmas, but to some extent we innocently brought the trouble on ourselves.

'I've been telephoned by the media and asked about the New Year's Eve party you attended,' a British Embassy official told me early in January. 'Do you realise that your costumes have been reported in the British press?'

I nodded. Penny and I had dressed up as 'The Midnight Express', she in a long black gown with a cardboard moon above her head and me as an express train.

'It was just a joke,' I muttered.

'Maybe but they are taking it to mean that you intend escaping.'

I gulped as he continued. 'I tried to tell them that it was a private function and that you had gone as private guests.'

However, we soon had more to worry about than silly hats. Months earlier, while were still locked up in the Sharifia police cells, those of us who had been at our party swapped ideas about what had happened.

A few of the group told me they intended to deny having had any alcohol to drink. I felt strongly opposed to this and said so.

'I think that's wrong,' I snapped irritably as they stared at me in surprise. 'What's the point of telling an untruth about something like that when we're facing a much more serious problem?' (At that time there was a chance we could be blamed, however unjustifiably, for the deaths of Helen and Johannes.)

'You don't admit anything in Saudi Arabia,' said one of the men who had been working there for some time.

'There's no point in telling lies,' I continued. 'If you tell lies about that, no one will believe you about anything else.'

The others just ignored me. As it turned out, those who claimed not to have been drinking were let off scot free.

In retrospect, I suppose I could have denied everything. I could have said that the alcohol had been brought by the guests, that I had not provided any intoxicating liquor. I could have told the police I was not drinking. Given the legal system, I could possibly have got off far more lightly.

But I saw no point in that; the others will live with the decisions they made. I will live with mine.

◧◩◨

We were accused of breaking Saudi laws, so we were due to face a sharia judge, and sharia procedure.

Sharia law evolved as an attempt to guide Muslims in the way in which God wants them to live. Based on the Koran, as well as the sayings of the prophet Mohammed, and others' recollections of him, sharia sets out to control more than does Western law. Sharia becomes involved with people's personal as well as public behaviour. Sharia's background is also rooted in local customary law, especially that dealing with commercial and criminal matters.

Judges of sharia law are trained in special schools, and they form part of a social elite that includes religious leaders, senior religious teachers, and scholars. There are different levels of sharia courts, much as our own judicial system ranges from magistrates' courts to supreme and courts of appeal. One rather democratic touch in Saudi Arabia is that any citizen has access to the king, and can appeal directly to him during a public audience the king holds almost daily.

Procedure in a sharia court is nothing like that of British and Australian courts. Most of the examination of the facts is carried out off stage so to speak. One is not necessarily entitled to speak in one's own defence. There are no legal counsel as we know them. Different status is accorded to witnesses; sometimes very little importance is placed on their evidence. Non-Muslims may not testify.

To outsiders, sharia has come to mean blood money, the axe, amputated hands, stoning, and the lash. Penny and I and Tim Hayter, and our German co-accused, were facing the last two of these.

◨◧◨

Our first court appearance took place on 9 January 1980. The court building was a squat, drab grey concrete building, a prototype government edifice. It could have been anywhere. A small flight of steps led from the dusty street into a vestibule, and then into our courtroom. The walls were pale green. The room was almost bare. There were none of the trappings one associates with the law in Britain or Australia, none of the black gowns and magnificent accoutrements designed to daunt the populace. Here, the only furniture was a simple table and chair for the judge, and some run of the mill plastic chairs which may have been intended for spectators, or people having business with the court.

In contrast to the usually immaculately attired Saudis, the judge, who was extremely fat, wore a crumpled and dirty *thobe*, with food stains down his front. His head dress, the *guttra*, was equally unkempt. The procedure was a formality, the judge merely reviewing our papers.

Our next appearance, on 16 February, was equally unsatisfactory. Proceedings took place entirely in Arabic. Our Saudi legal adviser, Dr al Sawaaf, was only permitted to attend the court as an interpreter. There was no mention of the deaths or private rights but we were told that Ron Smith had been sent a letter by the court informing him that, unless he claimed his private rights by a certain date, he would forfeit them and be ineligible for any blood money relating to his daughter's death. As far as I am aware, he never did respond.

Through the interpreter, Penny and Tim denied, as in their amended statements, that there had been any physical contact between them.

'Did you permit your wife to talk and dance with other men at the party?' I was then asked.

'This behaviour is acceptable in our culture,' I attempted to explain. 'It is commonplace.'

My answer was taken as indicating that I had given this permission.

At the same hearing, the Germans were asked whether they had consumed alcohol at the party.

Dieter Chapuis and Klaus Ritter admitted it. Penny and Tim and I admitted it.

◻卍◻

March 24 saw our third court appearance. That was a terrible day. Our case was heard by a single judge who had absolute authority.

We were judged solely on our signed statements. These were read out in Arabic and Dr al Sawaaf translated them.

Dieter Chapuis and Klaus Ritter, who had both admitted to drinking alcohol at the party, were each sentenced to a public flogging of thirty lashes. The other Germans, who had denied drinking, were given no further penalty and were discharged.

I held my breath as the remaining sentences were read out.

For changing their statements and for admitting to drinking alcohol, Penny and Tim were each sentenced to a public flogging of eighty lashes.

My crimes were listed as allowing the party to take place in my flat, having alcohol on the premises and serving it to guests, and allowing my wife to talk and dance with other men.

'One year in prison.'

I shook as I heard the words. One year in prison. How could that be? But there was more. For I had also admitted to drinking alcohol.

'Thirty lashes.'

The judge asked whether we accepted our penalties.

'No,' I said firmly, 'I think my sentence and my wife's sentence are unfair. All our sentences are unfair.'

We were led away.

Shake off the dust of Jeddah

'You must accept the sentences,' Dr al Sawaaf told me at the court after I protested. 'If you do not, the case will go to the intercession court where it will be re-opened and explored. That process will take months and you may receive stiffer sentences. You have received the lightest possible sentences. Please accept them.'

On his advice, I did. The secretary of the court also pointed out to Dr al Sawaaf that if he was unhappy with the verdicts, he could discuss the matter with Prince Naif ibn Abdul Aziz, the Minister for the Interior.

'I am very relieved, especially about Penny,' said Dr al Sawaaf as we left the court building. Francis Geere, the British consul, was more concerned about Penny's potential flogging than my prison sentence. He decided to team up with James Craig, the British Ambassador, to protest to Prince Naif about our sentences and that of Tim Hayter.

Strange times. Penny received a letter, postmarked Southampton, from 'The Salisbury Spanking Society'. I saw Idi Amin, from a distance, at a Saudi hotel. 'He's been given sanctuary here because he's a Muslim,' I told Penny, 'the murdering bastard.'

Back in England, the newspapers were having a field day. They pestered Penny's mother with questions, to all of which she answered, 'no comment'.

The British public were outraged at the sentences. They were shocked at the prospect of an Englishwoman being the first Western woman to be flogged. Jeddah opinion was against us though. 'The Saudis in the street are angry that you have got off so lightly,' Dr al Sawaaf informed us. 'They accuse you, Richard, of running a brothel.'

Dr al Sawaaf and the legal advisers for the Germans were pushing for further negotiations over the sentences. Over the next few weeks, Penny and I continued to meet with British Embassy officials and Dr al Sawaaf. Our hopes rose and fell.

Tim visited us one evening, soon after the sentencing. 'I've spoken to the Harms Salvage people,' he told us. 'We all agree that you should leave the country as soon as possible. We can lend you some money.'

'What about you?' asked Penny.

'I'm going to leave with the Germans. We can sail away in the tug at any time.'

Then, twenty-four hours later, Dr al Sawaaf greeted us warmly, looking his normal cheerful self. 'I have good news,' he beamed. 'I have just come from the British Ambassador. He has met with the Foreign Minister, Prince Sa'ad, who suggested that I meet with his deputy this week.'

This seemed a positive step.

'If you really want to leave the country, I can help you,' an employee of an import/export company told us.

'How?'

'By air freight. It's a foolproof method. We'll put you in a packing case and send you back to London by plane.'

Penny and I looked at one another.

'Don't worry,' continued the young man earnestly. 'We'll drill holes into the box so you'll be able to breathe properly.'

Foolproof? It seemed foolhardy to us. And I didn't like the man's slick manner. Did he know what he was talking about?

'No, of course not. You'd have to be totally mad to consider such a plan,' a pilot friend told us. 'For a start you don't know how long you will be in the packing case. How long will it sit around at the airport, here and in London?'

'Then there is an even bigger risk,' he went on. 'A lot of aircraft holds are not pressurised or heated. You could die of asphyxiation or freeze to death.'

◙|리|◙

The storming of the Grand Mosque in Mecca in November 1979 was the first unrelated event that might have affected the outcome of our trial. The second came in early 1980, hot on the heels of our final sentencing.

In Saudi Arabia, this second event was perceived as a direct insult by Britain to the royal house of al Saud. The British TV documentary 'Death of a Princess' told the story of the execution of a young and beautiful Saudi royal princess, Misha'il.

In the main square of Jeddah, in 1977, the young Princess Misha'il had been executed by firing squad. Her lover, Khalid Muhalhal, was then beheaded. They had had a fairly open affair in Jeddah, and later tried to elope. After they were arrested, Misha'il confessed to her adultery with Khalid, and later, defiantly, refused to retract. Her grandfather, Prince Muhammad Abdul Aziz, could have saved her, but was content to let her die in the name of family honour.

'Death of a Princess' showed Saudi life and law in a seriously unflattering light. Much of the film was held by the Saudi Arabian government to be an inaccurate and dramatised reconstruction. The Saudis tried very hard to prevent its being shown in the UK. They threatened to cut off diplomatic relations with Britain. Their ambassador was recalled from London. King Khalid himself threatened repercussions, especially on the English expatriates living and working in Saudi Arabia.

Penny's and my position vis à vis Saudi authority could hardly have been worse, even before the showing in Britain on 8 April of 'Death of a Princess'. And then Dr al Sawaaf told us that police intelligence branch knew we were drinking.

'You had better stop at once,' he advised.

I was furious at what I regarded as hypocrisy. I pointed out to Penny, 'Most of the Arabs drink. And we've all heard the stories – "Come and pick up your piano. It is leaking all over the port."

'Forget it, Richard,' was Penny's wise advice, 'we're in real trouble now over this television program.'

◻️⊏⊐◻️

Journalists continued to pester our friends and relations in England, offering to buy photographs and to pay for inside stories. We were news throughout the world, our story being reported in Greek and even Russian newspapers.

Dr al Sawaaf was still looking for a way out. 'You should accept the beatings,' he continued to advise, 'and ask for your prison sentence to be dropped, Richard. Then you will be immediately deported. It is a compromise but it could get you back home.'

We thought about it. The flogging was a ritual beating, we were told. Carried out with a cane on a clothed back, it was more a humiliation than anything else. The person inflicting the punishment had to have a copy of the Koran under his arm, so the resulting action was restrained. Women are seated while being flogged, although that may not necessarily help.

'It's no big deal,' I tried to reassure Penny, 'My Palestinian friend Morris had weekly floggings in prison, for ten years.'

◻️⊏⊐◻️

A couple of weeks later, in May, we were informed that Ron Smith had contacted Johannes Otten's parents and was stirring up the Dutch press. British television producers wrote, asking us to give a statement for use on a program based on Smith's allegations. If we agreed, the producers assured us, they would delay the screening until we returned to Britain.

—162—

'And if we don't agree, they'll go ahead without us,' Penny pointed out.

'That seems to be the inference. This is nothing short of blackmail,' I said.

We took the letter from the TV producer to Dr al Sawaaf who passed it on to the Saudi Ministry for Foreign Affairs. Dr al Sawaaf pointed out to them the pressure we were under and how keen we were to avoid excessive publicity.

The Foreign Affairs department's response was encouraging. 'The King's office is considering clemency and deportation,' Dr al Sawaaf told us the very next day, 'I am confident it will just be a matter of time.'

◻◿◻

At the start of June, Ron Smith returned to Jeddah. By then, the first anniversary of the deaths of Helen and Johannes had come and gone.

'Don't worry, Smith is only here to collect Helen's body,' Francis Geere assured me. But I was perturbed. We had heard of Smith's attempts to get a murder inquiry going. We heard, too, of rumours that had been circulating in England, tales of odd happenings at the party and the false assertion that Penny and Gordon Kirby had been having an affair before the party.

Helen Smith's body was flown back to Britain on 17 June 1980. Ron Smith followed a few days later, after he had made numerous visits and spoken to people all over Jeddah.

'He was searched by the police before he left,' a friend from the embassy told me. 'They confiscated all his notes, his films and his tapes. Goodness knows what information he has been gathering.'

Ron Smith's belongings were later returned to him. A front-page newspaper article in Britain quoted him as saying that the Saudi authorities had pledged to open an inquiry into his daughter's death, based on the data he had gathered.

Local information had it quite different. 'From all accounts the

Saudis were pretty unhelpful. They are not keen to have him here again, and encouraged him to leave as soon as possible,' was what we were told.

Nevertheless we were now seeing, first hand, just how obsessed Ron Smith was becoming with his daughter's tragic death, and how convinced he was that foul play had been involved.

Then we heard that a second post mortem was to take place.

'I must get someone to attend on our behalf,' I told Penny. I straight away telephoned a medical colleague of mine in Britain.

He reassured me. 'Don't worry, Richard. A Home Office pathologist is carrying out the post mortem. He is extremely competent.'

'But don't you think it is important for me to have someone independent present? After all, this post mortem has been instigated by Ron Smith. Would you be able to be there?'

'Richard, that won't be necessary. I'm sure it will be fine.'

As it turned out, that second post mortem on Helen Smith's body did indeed produce a straightforward result.

回르回

Despite Dr al Sawaaf's optimistic assurances, there did not appear to be any sign of forthcoming clemency and deportation. To depress us even further, it was suggested that the children be flown out to Saudi Arabia to be with us.

'No thank you,' I replied with all the politeness I could muster. 'We would prefer to return to them.'

Penny and I were introduced to the captain of a large pleasure boat which was travelling to Malta for a re-fit.

'Why don't you come out with me?' asked the American owner. 'I have a secret compartment where you can both hide. You will only have to stay there until we clear Saudi Arabian waters.'

We looked over the twenty-metre motor cruiser. His offer was very tempting.

'What do you think, Penny?' I asked. 'It seems like a good plan . . .'

'I'm scared. It seems like an extreme step to take.'

'I know, I know. But what's the alternative? For me to spend a year in prison and for you to be flogged? And we have no idea when the sentences will be carried out. We could be here for months and months. It's already been more than a year.'

Penny agreed. 'There's no end to this. I'm desperate to see the children, Richard. I'm so worried about them.'

'Well then, let's take a chance. I'm just not prepared to wait any longer.'

'All right.'

So we decided to meet the American on the beach at nine o'clock that night. We withdrew our money from the bank, packed our bags and bought some provisions for the trip. We were all set.

'Now we'd better go and tell Dr al Sawaaf that we're leaving and thank him for all his help,' I said.

Our minds made up, we walked into his office.

He opened his arms wide to greet us both. 'I have excellent news.'

'Actually we have some news for you,' I interrupted him. 'We have decided to leave, to escape in a boat tonight.'

'Please don't do that,' he said, 'you will wreck everything. I have heard from a very good source that you will soon be released.'

We believed him. We pulled out of our de luxe escape.

And still we waited. For days. For weeks. On again, off again. One day we thought we would be leaving the next. Then nothing. We were continually impatient and on edge. But there were some positive signs.

After more weeks of waiting, and worry about our punishments, Dr al Sawaaf got the news. The royal prerogative of mercy was to be exercised, but we must leave Saudi Arabia immediately. We were to pack our bags and board a plane bound for England, the following evening, Friday 8 August, coincidentally exactly one year to the day after Penny's release from Ruwais prison.

'Here are your tickets. Be at the airport by 10 p.m.,' we were told.

Our passports were still at Bakhsh Hospital.

'They can't be found. There may be a problem,' an official at the hospital informed me when I rang to ask for them.

'You're joking,' I shouted at him.

I then had to reassure Penny. 'There won't be any problem, I can promise you. We will not be stopped. We are allowed to leave and we are going to leave. I'll get the British Embassy to issue us with new passports.'

As with all other expatriates, our passports had been taken away on arrival in Saudi Arabia and we had been issued with a *batarga*, an ID card with photograph. This system meant the sponsor, the employer, had greater control over his employees; it was impossible to leave the country without a passport.

Most expatriates in Saudi Arabia, however, had wangled a second passport. How they managed that, I did not know, but one would have come in useful in our new predicament.

The embassy quickly came to our rescue. We went through formalities there and were able to show our new passports at the Sharifia police headquarters just in time. Our fingerprints and mug shots were taken yet again.

And what of our friends from the Harms Salvage Company? They, too, had been granted clemency. Most of the Harms people stayed working in Jeddah. Tim Hayter transferred to another company in another country. Jacques Texier went back to his caique in Obhor Creek and continued with his freelance diving. Martin Fleischer went back to Germany and resumed his interrupted university studies.

Penny and I were whisked through the airport so quickly that we did not have a chance to say goodbye to Dr al Sawaaf and his family who had come to bid us farewell.

At last, though, it was all behind us.

I settled back in my seat and sighed with relief as the aircraft took off. 'I am completely and utterly exhausted,' I murmured as Penny felt for the comfort of my arm.

'Me too,' and she glanced out of the window for one final

glimpse of Jeddah, the city lights sparkling in the dark night, 'thank goodness we made it.'

Although it was wonderful to be going home, I was experiencing a feeling of emptiness. It was an anticlimax, a bit like leaving prison. In gaol I had been cocooned from the pressures of the world. Now, again, I had to face up to reality. I had lived in a state of suspended animation for months in Saudi Arabia. Now I would have to look for a job; what were my prospects there? I had not practised surgery for about fifteen months. I had kept myself mentally alert, in the Ruwais prison library, reading textbooks and journals, but I had not actually worked as a doctor for over a year.

And flooding over me, my memories of Saudi Arabia, so full of paradox and contradiction: the scorn for petty theft, but the love of grand larceny; the asceticism of Bedouin desert life and the gross excesses of wealthy merchants; drunkenness in a country where alcohol is banned. The vast majority of Arabs I came to know as patients or as friends were delightful. They all had a good sense of humour, a great sense of honour and, most of all, generosity and hospitality that was breathtaking.

I remember one taxi driver who, when I hesitated at having him wait so I could use him for the return journey, offered me his car keys to take. He gave me his word by Allah that he would be in the same spot when I came back from my appointment.

Yet I hated the inefficiency, graft, greed and dishonesty of the country as a whole. I was often saddened to notice how cheap life seemed. The Saudis seemed, to me, to be particularly indifferent to the discomfort and suffering of others and had none of our preoccupations about death. I remember telling the son of one of my patients that his father had inoperable cancer and would soon die. The young man replied, '*Al hum du l'illah.*'

'Praise be to Allah.'

No place like home

London looked dismal at five o'clock in the morning, adding to my mood of despondency.

'Prepare yourself for the onslaught,' I told Penny as we were disembarking. We had been warned of a raucous media reception. But there was no one in wait. Not a soul.

'We have been spared,' I chuckled. 'What a blessed relief.'

As soon as we landed, I telephoned my mother to let her know we were back. Never one to waste words on the phone, she merely said, 'Darling, how wonderful that you are home at last,' and hung up.

Penny's mother came to Heathrow airport to collect us. She drove us back to her house in Trent, Dorset.

The children were waiting. We could hear their shrieks as soon as the car pulled up in the driveway.

'Mummy! Daddy!'

There was pandemonium – shouts and cries interspersed with laughter and tears. Penny was crying, I was crying, William was hugging me, Lucy was beside herself with joy. Meeting with my mother, and my brother Nick and his family was another rapturous reunion.

That afternoon the telephone rang. It was a London journalist who had got word that we were home. Within two hours, at least fifty reporters and photographers were camped out around the house. They arrived in one bunch, clutching notebooks, tape recorders, loaded down with cameras. A few knocked on the door. Others swarmed on the driveway or milled about on the lawn.

'Ignore them. They'll soon give up and go away,' suggested Penny.

'I doubt it. They're not going to move and we can't stay in the house for ever,' I replied, peeking through the curtains at the excited throng. 'We've got to talk to them sooner or later. Come on, let's get it over and done with,' I said.

I opened the front door and Penny and I strolled out on to the lawn as cameras flashed and powerful television lights were switched on. Blinking in the glare, I deflected all their questions.

'It is wonderful to be back,' I said, completely forgetting the attack I had intended to launch into.

'We are grateful to King Khalid for granting us clemency. Now we want to put this all behind us and get on with a normal life. We have not seen our children for over a year.'

I thanked them for their interest and asked to be left alone with our family. Fat chance. At that stage we still hadn't any idea of the dreadful battering we were to receive at the hands of the British media. Nor did we anticipate how often we would long for the peace and stillness of life in Jeddah and its efficient press censorship.

The following day, our return was front page news in every daily newspaper. We were mentioned on every radio and television broadcast. Haggard-looking mug shots from Jeddah flashed into every household in the country.

The village of Trent, with its glorious old buildings dating back to the sixteenth century, is set in a little hollow surrounded by hills. The local community was close knit and their focal point was The Rose and Crown with its welcoming atmosphere, the sort of pub that people would travel fifty kilometres to for a beer and a sandwich. We felt comfortable in Trent. But the small village was almost taken over by the intruders. Our every move was dogged by the press. We were followed everywhere we went. 'Imagine how we would have been hounded if we had escaped,' Penny said to me.

'Take our car,' offered some friends, 'and get away for a while.'

So, early one morning, without telling a soul, we set off, managing to evade the waiting posse of newshounds. We drove to Scotland and spent a relaxing week or two in a small hotel on the west coast. There we came to a decision.

'We're going to have to tell our story, Richard, and end this harassment.'

'Yes, it seems the only way.'

We sold our story to the *Daily Mail*. We ignored friendly warnings. We were paid 10 000 pounds. We badly needed the money. By then, I had not been able to work for nearly a year and a half.

'We want to have the final say over what is published,' I told them.

'Fine.'

We were interviewed by Ann Leslie and Harry Longmuir. Five articles appeared during late September and early October.

To me, the stories appeared frivolous and lightweight. 'Listen to this. They've made a really big deal about the movie we watched on the flight home.'

'What was it?'

'Something called *Dirty Money*. They are making the connection that we went out to Saudi Arabia as mercenaries, and that watching this film was very appropriate.'

The *Daily Mail* let us see the first four of the articles before they went to print. However, when it was time for the fifth and final piece, Ann and Harry were sorry, 'We're running out of time. We're on a deadline, Richard. We can't show you this one first.'

'That's okay.'

It wasn't. 'They gave us their word this wouldn't happen,' I seethed. 'We trusted them and look what they've done to us.'

Penny felt badly let down. 'It's horrid. They claim that we have not been telling the truth. How can they say that?'

We had tried to be frank about everything with the two journalists. The only detail we kept to ourselves was the story about Penny and Tim. That was too private.

I felt enraged and betrayed. Was it worth the 10 000 pounds we received? I think not. Certainly we had the much-needed money but, in telling our story, we had helped to inflame the doubts and suspicions circulating about the party.

In my time as a young intern and surgeon, I used to enjoy reading *Private Eye*. It had been founded in 1962 to punish pomposity and to scourge the establishment. Like most of my friends I lapped up its mixture of satire, comedy and what I believed at the time were serious investigations. As a matter of fact, I still have a look at it from time to time. Now, though, I read *Private Eye* much more circumspectly.

Whatever its enemies claim, the press is a bastion of our social and political freedoms, and *Private Eye* has been second to none in questioning and probing British business and political leaders for nearly forty years. However, pity help you if you find yourself an innocent object of the attention of the satirical journal.

The deaths of Helen Smith and Johannes Otten were a great loss to their families and others who loved them. The tragedy was compounded by their youth and the cruel manner of their deaths. Except perhaps for some prurient passers-by, I was the first person to examine their bodies, and to call for police and ambulance. I know exactly what I saw on the Jeddah street that morning, and what caused it. I was and am a trained and experienced doctor of medicine. There could hardly have been anyone better qualified to assess on the spot how Helen and Johannes died.

Yet, shortly after Penny and I returned to England, *Private Eye* got a bee in its bonnet, and decided that the simple truth was a lie and that some kind of cover-up was under way.

I still find it hard to understand how an apparently intelligent organisation like *Private Eye* could have been seduced into waging a campaign that lasted for years, and roped in all sorts of people including the Foreign Secretary, the Attorney-General, British Intelligence, the entire Saudi government, even a life insurance company. And of course, there was me. And Penny.

To this day we have no idea who were our accusers. Without any parallel in modern journalism (except perhaps in Liberia), all stories in *Private Eye* are published anonymously. The names of the proprietor(s), editor, cartoonists, and even some satire contributors are public knowledge. But the bulk of the writers conceal themselves behind innocuous pseudonyms: Gnome, HP Sauce, Grovel, the Street of Shame. The magazine refers to itself in the third person, cutely, as 'The Eye'. The writing is given to petty-bourgeois English disdain for working people, querying once why I would have held a party for a bunch of 'drunken sweaty divers'.

Experienced journalists are thought to be difficult to convince about conspiracies and plots. Notwithstanding, *Private Eye* leapt to attack soon after Penny and I were pardoned and released by the Saudi government.

Whether they were attracted by Ron Smith's so-called crusade, I have no way of knowing. Soon after their series of articles began, though, *Private Eye* mentioned that Ron Smith had used a concealed tape recorder in his conversations with me. I certainly hadn't told them that, so maybe Ron Smith did. That Ron Smith decided to tape our conversation the very first time he met me did not seem to arouse the suspicions of the writers of *Private Eye*. Years later, I still believe Ron Smith's action was underhand.

I suppose too, given the xenophobic mindset of *Private Eye* in those days, the disdain of the Saudi police and officials for Ron Smith would have helped to confirm Smith's value in the journalists' eyes.

So the long campaign got under way. In one of the very first items about Helen's death, *Private Eye* sneeringly referred to Penny as a sex siren; and falsely claimed she was a drug addict. According to the item, Penny and I were at the centre of a secret wife-swapping circle (we had been in Jeddah for a whole twenty weeks). On top of that, Penny was having an affair with one of the officials from the British Embassy. This later turned out to be the baseless story regarding Penny and Gordon Kirby, over which Kirby would sue *Private Eye* for libel. So *Private Eye* told its readers. And there was more; Johannes Otten had been set upon and stabbed to death by the German divers, who had then carefully carried him downstairs and impaled him on the railings to conceal the knife wounds. (The British will believe anything of the Germans.) Helen had a wardrobe fall on her, and then she was chucked out the window.

A couple of issues later, to keep public interest aroused, Lord Carrington, the Foreign Secretary, was portrayed on the cover saying, according to the one of the famous *Private Eye* cod dialogue bubbles . . . something nasty about foreigners that I cannot now repeat for fear of ending up arraigned by the Race Relations Board.

Subsequently, *Private Eye* generously informed its readers that I was not drunk the night of the party ('as reported in our last issue'). They were not going to let me off altogether; the item went on to reveal a Saudi judge had announced to Ron Smith that 'Richard Arnot [is] "the devil incarnate"'.

Then in quick succession came the news that Helen and I were lovers; but confusingly that Helen was in love with an Iranian paediatrician, who had a wife and children back in Teheran. There followed the sign that a conspiracy theorist looks for; the paediatrician had disappeared back to Teheran hours after Helen died – at the behest of the Bakhsh Hospital. The magazine also published a lengthy Foreign Office denial of all the allegations (with interpolated *Private Eye* comments). As an aside they included the claim we had not gone near the bodies of Helen and Johannes for an hour after being told they were lying in the street.

Gordon Kirby from the British Embassy was a subject of great interest to *Private Eye*. For months the writers insisted that he was having an affair with Penny, until eventually he sued for libel. *Private Eye* promptly launched an appeal for funds to fight the case. (Much later they diverted the small sum they collected to Ron Smith.)

A great deal of *Private Eye*'s information they claimed came from staff at the Bakhsh Hospital. Fair enough that some of it was supposed to be from nurses who may have known us at work or socially. But *Private Eye* often quoted kitchen staff as well. I still do not know why they were thought to know so much about me; I did not live in the hospital, and I seldom ate the food there. I didn't so much as recognise some of the names of people who claimed to *Private Eye* to be such good buddies that they knew whom I was sleeping with.

From the Foreign Office to MI6 is a logical step when you are expounding a conspiracy theory. That we had been hosted by the de Klees, and that they had been exceptionally kind to us throughout our time in Jeddah was used merely to demonstrate that Colonel Murray de Klee, military attaché, therefore suspected MI6, must have been in the cover-up, too.

As far as I can guess, the plot which I was supposed to be part of went something like this. After the BBC TV documentary, 'Death of a Princess', exploded across Saudi-UK relations, any further scandal would have brought diplomatic and commercial contacts nearly to breaking point. That would have impeded arms sales (a major UK export), and other defence and business ties between our two countries. Plot theorists believed (I think) that Helen and Johannes had met their deaths as a result either of expatriate workers murdering them, or Saudis murdering them. British intelligence, the Foreign Office, Saudi police, and judiciary had hastened to conceal the cause of death, and tried to pass off the so-called murders as an accident. Penny and I, British spies, were involved in the cover-up. Others, the good people, namely *Private Eye*, Ron Smith, and the Bakhsh Hospital cook, were fighting to reveal the truth.

At about this point, pathologists' reports began to make up a good deal of the *Private Eye* coverage. That Helen's poor remains had been returned to the UK stripped entirely of internal organs, lungs, heart, digestive tract, and so on might, one would hope, reduce experts' urge to pontificate about the cause of death. That her body had been filled with a mixture of charcoal, sawdust and moth balls, and kept in a refrigerator for a couple of years does not seem to have brought about any doubt as to ability to detect bruising, or decide the cause of other external marks. Her body was so badly disfigured, that one pathologist denied the existence of an appendicectomy scar, the result of an operation that I had carried out myself.

In a fairly standardised statement, one of the pathologists decided that injuries to Helen would have been caused by a fall from 'thirty feet [nine metres] or more'. Fair enough. In other words, to sustain damage of a particular nature, a text book of forensic pathology would tell you that a person would have to fall more than thirty feet. *Private Eye* quoted this statement accurately, once. But perhaps the writers did not understand the statement's prescriptive nature. In future issues, the figure shrank to simply 'thirty feet'. Later, when the Iranian paediatrician was discovered batching on the first floor, the victims did not have far to fall at all. Yet another investigator later pronounced that they had been hurled from the roof, which was even further up than our balcony.

Some of my best friends are forensic pathologists. But in Australia, which saw a visiting (English) expert, who would not recognise a dingo if it walked up and licked him on the leg, send a woman to gaol for the death of her baby, because he claimed to have seen a pattern like the Turin shroud on the child's jacket, scepticism is rife.

Unfortunately *Private Eye* took notice of too many expert theories. Quite likely, their own native intelligence, if they had used it, would have made them wonder how much information should be derived from a much-handled cadaver after years in a deep freeze.

Rather than that, *Private Eye* discovered a new and extraordinary pathology theory, according to which Helen's body had fallen 'maybe only a few feet'; 'her body was badly battered by blows'; and 'her thighs [were] battered as though she had been sexually, and roughly, assaulted'. Soon, Helen's death due to falling twenty metres from the sixth-floor balcony was transformed by *Private Eye* to 'if there was a fall at all'.

In support of Ron Smith, *Private Eye* were urging the Smiths' local authority, West Yorkshire, to hold an inquest. It would have been a fair enough request in most circumstances. The only reasons not to hold an inquest seemed to be that the Saudis had run a lengthy inquiry of their own, and that very little could be decided on the sketchy evidence still available from Helen's body.

The county's hesitation only increased the allegations of conspiracy and cover-up. The powers-that-be of West Yorkshire were very resolute in their determination not to inquire into Helen's death. The noisy criticism of their refusal went on for months. As a bystander, of course, I (or rather, we) suffered collateral damage from *Private Eye*'s fortnightly outbursts. I was categorised as an obscure doctor, who had been co-opted into the Yorkshire aristocracy (Penny's family). The church where we were 'magnificently' married, Wakefield Cathedral, represented to *Private Eye* another sign that something must be going on.

Then, hot off the typewriters, another allegation. It seemed that when I operated on Helen for appendicitis, I had actually been performing an abortion. This they claimed was told to Helen's father in Malaysia.

Private Eye complained that Gordon Kirby's legal fees for his suit against them for libel were being paid by the Foreign Office. They thought it unfair that civil servants who were libelled while performing their public tasks should receive public money to defend themselves. Of course, if Kirby had not happened to be working in the embassy in Jeddah at the time of our arrest, he would never have found himself publicly accused of adultery.

That at the same time Ron Smith was granted legal aid in his campaign for an inquest, as far as the High Court and then further, to the Court of Appeal, did not seem an equally extravagant waste of government money to *Private Eye*'s anonymous writer(s).

The economic weapon was being deployed on many fronts at this time. The West Yorkshire Coroner, Philip Gill (in his official capacity), was denied funds by his county council to fight the case in the High Court against an inquest brought by the publicly subsidised Ron Smith. For some reason to do with English practice, the county's chief coronial official had to pay the costs from his own pocket.

Philip Gill 'is well-heeled'. 'Fortunately, he can afford it,' crowed *Private Eye*. They made much that week, too, of Philip Gill having the bad luck to come 'by curious coincidence' from 'the next village' to

Penny's family. Philip Gill's 'extended' holiday in Fiji at about that time was also thought worth a mention by *Private Eye*.

Another way of disseminating a rumour, probably not all that new, and certainly not subtle, was demonstrated by a note at the foot of an item about Ron Smith's High Court case. This is how it went; 'Someone wrote to "The Eye" a few weeks ago with the interesting news [sic] that Dr Arnot did not spend the night of Helen Smith's death in his flat, but was in the Bakhsh hospital. Please will this person write to us again, making himself or herself known.'

The ranks of the conspirators widened further. 'Something very serious seems to be wrong with Lord Justice Ormrod and Mr Justice Forbes' . . . 'All the legal and case authority since 1887 suggests . . . But Lord Justice Ormrod whose job it is to interpret acts of Parliament – not reverse them – coolly set the specific provision . . . aside' . . . 'It would be comfortable to conclude from all this that . . . the law is an ass and that Lord Justice Ormrod and Mr Justice Forbes are living proofs . . . the cover up which until now has been masterminded by the Foreign Office with a little help from the Home Office – has now recruited the judiciary.'

Private Eye were doing some recruiting of their own at the time, in the form of a life insurance company. German employers, such as Harms Salvage, insure all their workers against death or injury in the course of their duties. When the time came to pay death benefits to Johannes Otten's parents, Roelofs, an underwriting company, refused, saying that they had heard there was a fight, and drinking (at a party!), and that Johannes had contributed to his own demise. *Private Eye* seemed to believe that it was significant, or unusual, that an insurance company might try to avoid paying out on a claim. To *Private Eye* at this point, it appeared, even a parsimonious insurance firm was a useful ally.

Soon after the judges of the High Court were 'recruited' into the cover-up, they were joined by the Attorney-General, Sir Michael Havers. He, it seems, was 'MP for Richard and Penelope Arnot when they lived in Wimbledon before leaving for Saudi Arabia'.

In the same item *Private Eye* went on to tell its readers that *Le Matin* ran an article in its colour supplement that 'alleges an intelligence background to the nurse's death. Richard Arnot . . . was working for British intelligence, and Johannes Otten . . . was working for Dutch intelligence'.

The barmy allegations were coming in torrents by now; 'Regan is not related to the Arnots, but his wife Jane's sister, Judy, was a very close friend of the Arnots in Jeddah'. This pearl came in a very long *Private Eye* quotation from an article in the Devon *Sunday-Independent* entitled 'How Helen Smith Really Died'. It had been written by someone called Simon Regan, whose family tree I have just quoted. The story concluded that Johannes was thrown from the roof of our block. And this time it was Helen's body that was carried all the way down the stairs. But not by Germans. On this occasion, it was the Arabs. Foreigners anyway. Whichever *Private Eye* investigator wrote up the latest version, seems to have lost track of all the forensic theories which a fortnight before they were trumpeting; that maybe the bodies had not fallen at all; that wardrobes had fallen; that Germans had been stabbing away in fights, and so on.

◧⼳◨

On one occasion, I went to the offices of *Private Eye* in Soho. I didn't ring first. I wanted to speak to them in person. At the tiny office, a sole staff member, a female receptionist was busily polishing her nails, and showed not the slightest hint of recognition nor interest in me.

'I would like to speak with the editor, Mr Richard Ingrams, please.'

'He's away at a meeting in the country.'

'When will he be back?'

'I don't know,' she replied, listlessly.

'Would you be kind enough to let him know that Richard Arnot called to see him and that I would like to arrange to meet. Here are my contact details.'

I never heard a word from him.

At another time, I considered suing *Private Eye*. The late Sir James Goldsmith, who was also suffering at their hands, offered to bear 90 per cent of my legal costs.

My London solicitor, Sir David Napley, persuaded me otherwise. '*Private Eye* are very experienced in this field, Richard,' he told me.

'But I have a good case,' I protested. 'They allege I was responsible for Helen's death.'

'I know, but they will extract every scrap of titillation from the proceedings. It will be a saga that will take months, if not years, to sort out,' Sir David pointed out. 'They will go into your background, every little aspect of your life. You can give up any idea of getting back into serious surgery. Your whole life will be taken up with a court case like that, and for a very long time.'

My lawyer brother Nick was equally pessimistic about court action. 'Every edition of *Private Eye* is set up as a separate company. Each company has about a shilling in the bank. It's futile to sue the magazine. And a libel suit would take a terrible toll of your time and energy,' he told me.

Private Eye seemed to have considerable reach, too. A few weeks after returning to Britain, Penny and I were questioned by the West Yorkshire Metropolitan Police, a formality we were assured, in case of any coronial inquiry.

'The whole circumstances of this affair would seem to be highly suspicious to an observer,' began the Detective Chief Inspector who was interviewing us. 'I would have thought that sea captains and deep sea divers were not in your particular social level.'

Ah, the arrogance of the British and the divisiveness of the class system. I was further astonished when he based his questions on items that had appeared in *Private Eye*.

'I read to you from an article dated 15 August 1980. "Penny and Richard Arnot were at the centre of a secret wife-swapping circle in Jeddah." Is there any truth in that?'

'That is totally untrue,' I replied.

'Here is another paragraph. "One of Penny Arnot's lovers was Foreign Office diplomat George Kirby, vice-consul at the Jeddah embassy. It was Kirby who was summoned to the scene shortly after dawn on 20 May 1979 when the bodies had been discovered, following that all-night orgy in the surgeon's flat. Kirby, whose own wife worked at a British-run medical clinic in the commercial capital, pumped his mistress full of black coffee in a desperate attempt to sober up the hysterical creature before the Saudi police arrived." Any truth in that?'

'None. As I've already said, I only met Mr Kirby for the first time on the morning of 20 May 1979,' answered Penny.

Undeterred, the policeman continued reading from the article.

'Here it states "Helen, it is alleged, came to grief within the flat either by being bounced upon or crushed by a heavy wardrobe falling on her; her dead or unconscious body was then tossed from the balcony of the fifth floor apartment.

' "The official version is that Helen and Otten fell from the balcony while making love and a post mortem examination in Leeds indicated that Helen's death was accidental. The more probable version of Helen's fate, however, is in part supported by two witnesses who separately described hearing one, just one horrible thud. This was undoubtedly when a single body struck the ground, but surprisingly both witnesses say that no cry or scream preceded the thud."

'Did you in the course of that night hear a horrible thud, Mr Arnot?'

'No.'

The Detective Chief Inspector continued. 'The article concludes with this: "While the Arnots holiday and dream of the money the film rights could produce from the richly embroidered tale of their heroic suffering in Saudi Arabia, the General Medical Council may care to reflect on a surgeon who just before he was due to perform major surgery was hopelessly drunk on near 100 proof homebrewed spirit".'

'I emphatically deny the allegations made in that paragraph,' I snapped back at him.

What more indignity and humiliation were we to suffer? I was no longer locked up in a grubby little cell in appalling conditions, shackled in handcuffs whenever I was taken anywhere, but this line of questioning by British police was equally degrading and ignominious.

Private Eye was against us, but did not seem to worry who else they lumped in with us. Even poor Helen was claimed to have had affairs with everyone from the cleaning staff of the Bakhsh Hospital, to a paediatric specialist. And, of course, me.

Other newspapers defended us, or at least refrained from printing every rumour, and every furphy. The *Times*, the *Daily Telegraph*, and to some slight extent, the *Daily Mail*, covered our problems fairly. The tabloids and the *Guardian* went for the gossip and the conspiracies. I have always had balanced coverage in the Australian media.

◻️⟳◻️

If we thought we were in for understanding and an easy ride back in the UK, we were seriously deluding ourselves.

I did not look forward to returning to work in the National Health Service. I did not like the way it ran – people spending hours in grievously understaffed and overcrowded outpatient clinics, doctors unable to practise very good medicine because they had to rush to get through their quota of patients. I found it all disillusioning. I had not trained for ten years as a surgeon in order to work under those conditions. I wanted to do something better.

As it turned out, I had little chance of a job anyway. I had been rejected by the medical fraternity.

'How did your meeting go?' asked Penny one afternoon, after I had tried my professional colleagues again.

'Don't ask,' I replied. 'I've spoken with several surgeons and they have convinced me that my professional future is hopeless here. Things are not looking good.'

Winter was coming. The weather was cold and lousy. We had no money and no job prospects. Everything was going downhill.

'Why don't you try America?' suggested my one remaining good friend among my professional colleagues. 'I'll write you a letter of introduction to Charles Robb.' One of Britain's most highly respected surgeons, Robb had moved away from the progressive destruction of the National Health system some years earlier and transferred to the Rochester School of Medicine in Minnesota.

Armed with my friend's letter and a surge of optimism, I boarded a plane to America in October. Now I was cut loose from my restraints once more, and seeking a new life.

The wide brown land

In the United States, I attended a surgical conference, made several contacts and met with Charles Robb. He, in turn, introduced me to another professor of surgery who offered me a position at the Lutheran Hospital in Brooklyn, which I was delighted to accept.

'You do realise that you will have to sit the American board's examination and work as a hospital resident for four years before you can become a registered consultant surgeon here,' the professor told me.

A lawyer started on my application for permanent residency in the United States. 'It will take at least six months for your visa to be processed,' he told me.

So this was to be my new home, New York, the Big Apple. I was apprehensive. Travelling to the Lutheran Hospital on the subway was frightening. Everyone looked strange and menacing. There was the feeling of latent violence wherever I went.

My new sponsor lived in a smart apartment block, not far from where John Lennon had been shot dead the year before. I was startled to see a loaded automatic 12-gauge shotgun leaning near his front door. 'It's just a normal security precaution,' he explained casually, 'to discourage any uninvited guests.'

I returned to England in November, wondering how to fill in my time usefully until my visa was approved in June. My confidence was at an all-time low. I had not performed any operative surgery for almost two years. I needed a locum job.

Penny's last words to me before I had left for the States were, 'Get yourself sorted out, Richard.'

'What about our relationship? Where do we stand?' I had asked.

'Listen, Richard, you have to sort yourself out before we can talk about that. Decide what you are going to do. Find a job. I'm staying here, where I have a home and family.'

During those few months back in the UK, Penny and I had re-established our relationship. Difficult circumstances brought us together and we were closer than ever. We had not talked any further about separating, and my hopes remained high of a good and lasting marriage.

Penny was still living at her mother's home in Trent. William and Lucy had settled well into the excellent local school. I spent much of my time in London, only returning to Dorset at weekends. Would Penny come to live in America with me, with the children? It was too early to make those plans, she told me; she was still considering our relationship.

Encouraged by a couple of journalists, we decided to write a book on our experiences. One of the two, Tim Sisley, worked on the local newspaper. I began to put my story down on tape. Tim began working on that. John Close, an American, the other helper, was in England and collaborating with Penny on the book. Penny and I knew John's parents, Ray and Marty, in Jeddah. We had stayed at their place for a short time during our house arrest. That was how Penny met John, who was working as a journalist for the local *Arab News*.

In the meantime, my career was in tatters. My first objective must be to get back to some sort of professional life. Then I could concentrate on my marriage. I needed to refresh my medical skills before I went permanently to the United States. I worked out some options.

First, I settled down with my family for a cold and miserable Christmas in Dorset. Christmas made all the more miserable by a third post mortem carried out on the body of Helen Smith in

December by a Danish pathologist, Dr Joergen Dalgaard, hired by Ron Smith. My time in prison had left me with a legacy. After my spell there, I had a far greater certainty about some issues, and I learnt to trust my hunches. I now felt strongly that there should be an independent witness at this autopsy, but I did not follow it up. I should have. The third post mortem came up with eccentric findings that were to cause many future problems.

◫◫◫

In mid-January, a Sydney locum service that employed overseas doctors offered me a job, a work permit, and an air ticket booked two weeks later, at the end of January.

As soon as I stepped off the plane in Sydney, my fatigue lifted. I had a remarkable feeling of having come home, even though I had only ever spent two days in Sydney, in 1966, during my time as ship's surgeon on the SS *Canberra*.

Everything was familiar and reassuring to me, reminiscent of my childhood in Africa: the evening light, so clear and bright after the perpetual haze of England, the accents, the smells, the atmosphere, right down to the clothes people wore.

At the airport inquiry counter, I asked about accommodation. 'I'm looking for somewhere cheap and by the sea.'

'The Astra Hotel at Bondi should suit you, sir. Would you like the $10 or the $20 room?'

'The $10 room will be fine.'

My cab driver was equally friendly and efficient. A part-time university student, he was most interested about what I was doing in Sydney. I told him of the plans for my three-month working holiday, mentioning the name of the locum agency that had organised my job.

He fell silent.

'Is there anything wrong?' I asked.

'It's probably none of my business,' he said, 'but from what I've heard, they're not too good.'

That sounded like trouble; I had moved half way around the world to meet up with another disreputable employer.

'What's wrong with them?'

'I share a flat with a doctor who used to work for that outfit. The company overcharges the government for doctors' services. A number of them, mainly the overseas ones, are now facing fraud charges.'

That was all I needed. The thought of legal hassles, after what I had been through in the last two years, put me right off that locum agency.

'No, mate, I wouldn't work for that mob if I were you,' he told me as we pulled up at the entrance to the Astra.

I was so perturbed by what he had told me I could hardly appreciate the view of the rolling surf and the gleaming beach. I paid him a handsome tip, realising he had just done me an enormous good turn. Of all the taxi drivers in Sydney, I had encountered the one who could save me from possible disaster.

The next day, at the offices of the Australian Medical Association; 'I'm not really allowed to say too much,' the receptionist informed me, 'but they do not have a very good reputation.'

That was all I needed. I found the address of another agency and through them accepted a GP locumship in the country town of Condobolin, in western New South Wales. There I fell in love with rural practice. I was nominally a locum GP, but there was no surgeon in the town, and my surgical skills were soon put to the test, with some trepidation on my part as, by this time, I had not wielded a scalpel for nearly two years.

My medical training was not deficient but my unfamiliarity with the Australian vernacular caused a few hiccups. During my first week in Condobolin I asked a station hand how he had acquired the large blisters on his hands and he answered 'fencing'.

'Is there much fencing done in the area?' I asked eagerly.

'Sure, doc, with this drought, almost everyone is fencing. There is nothing else to do.'

My mind teemed with visions of station hands cavorting about the paddocks in pairs, sword or rapier in hand, calling out 'touché'.

'What do you use?' I asked.

'Oh, you know, the usual,' he replied, 'barbed wire, droppers, posts.' I turned away to blush.

The following day, a farmer confused me when she described her condition, 'I'm crook and getting crooker.' Later she informed me, 'I felt a right dill, doc, fair dinkum I did.'

When I asked her what her husband did, she told me, 'He shot through years ago.'

◧◩◩

Two weeks after starting my locum, I rang Penny and asked her to take the next flight over with the children.

'You'll love it here,' I enthused. I was increasingly certain that my future lay in this friendly and welcoming country.

'But what about America?' she asked.

'I don't know, come and see what you think.'

The lifestyle of a country doctor seemed ideal to me – trading in the hassles of a city life for the chance of living out in the wide open spaces, perhaps on a small farm, maybe even flying again. There was a shortage of surgeons in country towns. Things were getting better by the minute.

She told me she had no intention of living in Australia, but Penny agreed to give it a go. (Another new expression I had picked up.) Soon afterwards she and William and Lucy arrived in Condobolin for what I, probably naively, hoped would be the beginning of a new life together.

Quickly, our marriage settled into the old familiar pattern of quarrels, long silences, short-lived reconciliation, arguments about money.

Penny soon discovered that, in her words, the shopping in outback New South Wales is fine if you want barbed wire or sheep drench. It is indeed a long way from Sloane Street. A few spiders

—187—

hanging about in our cramped quarters and clouds of flies in the garden were the clinchers.

Penny decided country life was not for her and the children.

Our marriage had been disintegrating through all our misadventures. I had tried to hold it together because I dreaded losing daily contact with William and Lucy. Like many others have had to, I had to admit it was all over.

Our goodbyes at the airport were civil.

'I'm going to speak to the *Daily Telegraph* in Sydney,' I told her.

'What on earth for?'

'Because I want to stay here and I want to set the record straight about what happened in Jeddah. Friends have suggested this is the thing to do.'

'Some friends. Why do you want to bring all of that up again?'

My interview with the *Telegraph* ended up as a very balanced article and they added an editorial ending with the recommendation that Australia give us 'a fair go'.

'The country needs surgeons with your training and experience,' I was told by a high-ranking surgeon. After the disdain and total lack of support I had received from fellow surgeons in England, his words were music to my ears.

◻️🉐◻️

By 1981 I was living happily in Inverell, a thriving town of 10 000 people on the New England plateau of New South Wales. I had found work as a GP surgeon in a group practice and had signed on as Visiting Medical Officer at the local hospital.

On my first working day, 5 July 1981, I paid a visit to a car showroom to negotiate the purchase of a new vehicle. Switching on the car radio, the salesman found the local announcer in the middle of announcing my arrival in town, referring to the Jeddah affair.

Was I ever going to get away from that business?

Soon, though, I realised the truth of the adage, 'there is no such thing as bad publicity'. My first week in practice saw me far busier than the medical problems on display warranted. I suspect that a lot of people were curious to see me on account of the notoriety surrounding the party in Jeddah. Later, a number of those early patients became good friends and they and their families have been loyal patients ever since.

Until I came to work in Australia, I had no intention of becoming a country surgeon. Indeed, on the face of it, my surgical training had been specifically directed towards an academic position in a teaching hospital equipped with facilities where I could put into practice my training in vascular, oncological and major gastrointestinal surgery. I had taken two years off from clinical surgery for my research and had written a major thesis and been awarded a Master of Surgery. I had worked for three consultants with extensive vascular practices and had specialised in the surgical treatment of cancer for two years while working as senior surgical registrar at London's Royal Marsden Hospital.

But there had been a few pointers along the way. Visiting Newfoundland as a medical student, I had been impressed by the multidisciplinary clinics in isolated areas. Psychologically, I was more suited to a provincial practice. During my two years in London, I used to spend almost every weekend driving out of the city, for a breath of country air and country life. Now I had a country practice and a country life. In Inverell.

In the process I met a wonderful woman, Margaret Johnson, who was to become my future wife. A teacher for the profoundly deaf, she was a very sensible and straightforward person with a good sense of humour and a lovely smile. Of slim build, her blue eyes were a very attractive combination with her jet black hair. I was pretty lonely in those days and she was exactly the sort of person I was looking for. She had a sort of constancy and was very forthright and honest.

We got to know one another gradually and, the more time I spent with Margaret, the more certain I became that this was the woman with whom I wanted to share my life. Finally, at Noosa Heads, while we were having dinner at a restaurant, I asked her to marry me.

◨⯐◧

Penny and I had been divorced in June 1982, on the grounds of irretrievable breakdown of our marriage. My great regret was the loss of the children who opted to remain living with her in the USA. I have kept in touch and William and Lucy visit me in my new home, but there was some friction and William especially found it hard to forgive what he considered to be my abandonment of them.

For my part, I missed them greatly. I felt destitute without them. I always enjoyed my children although, looking back, I guess I didn't show it very much at the time.

My day in court

In mid 1982 came the telephoned announcement that was to take my life back to the events of Jeddah again. The call was from England, from a journalist in Fleet Street. 'Mr Arnot, have you heard that the Leeds coroner has agreed to hold an inquest into the death of Helen Smith?'

'No, I haven't.'

'Will you be attending?'

I did not hesitate for a moment. 'Of course I will be attending if I am asked to go,' I responded. 'I'll go. No question about it.'

He seemed somewhat taken aback. 'Will your former wife be attending?' he asked after a moment.

'I don't know, you'll have to ask her that. But I certainly will be coming over if any inquest is to be held.'

Why was I so sure? For one important reason. I saw this as my public duty. I have been asked since whether I wanted to attend in order to clear my name. No, that didn't affect my decision in the slightest. On the other hand, if I had not attended, people would have wondered what I had to hide.

My brother, Nick, a lawyer in England, was more cautious. 'If you do come over, you must be legally represented,' he advised.

'You know Ron Smith has made repeated allegations on all manner of things, including your involvement in Helen's death. You must be legally represented. There is no question about it.'

I took heed of Nick's words. Two years younger than me, he was a senior partner in a legal practice. He had successfully shielded my mother from unpleasant publicity after Penny and I were first arrested.

Nick's were wise words. My experience of inquests had only been as a medical professional – a day or two of hearings, and then, 'Thank you, doctor, that will be fine'. This was the usual manner of things. I now imagined I would go to England, give my evidence and be back in time for lunch.

Nick soon put me right. 'This is going to be huge. It will take ages. Ron Smith has been badgering the authorities for this for years.'

It was not as if I had entirely escaped noticing Ron Smith's efforts for an inquest to be held during my time in Australia. Doggedly persistent, he had flown to Kuala Lumpur in June of the previous year to interview Guruswami, his daughter's Malaysian boyfriend. Beneath headlines such as 'Father chases "killer"' and 'Father closes in on killer', British and Australian newspapers documented his travels and his allegations.

Ron Smith told reporters in Kuala Lumpur that he had 'damning new evidence' on his daughter's death and that the killer, whom he described as 'a British aristocrat' was in Australia. Smith intended to fly to Sydney to confront the man whom he said had murdered his daughter at the party in Saudi Arabia two years before. The killer, claimed Ron Smith, was being protected by the British government which did not want details of the 'Jeddah orgy' to be made public. 'People like Mrs Thatcher (the British Prime Minister), and Lord Carrington (the Foreign Secretary) are covering up for this man. That's why he was shifted out of England and has been moved from country to country,' he was reported as saying. Smith claimed that he had been trailing the man around the world. 'He slipped into Australia about nine weeks ago from Los Angeles,' he said.

I responded indignantly. 'Now I'm angry enough to hit back,' I told the papers. 'My family have suffered an incredible unending nightmare . . . My former wife Penny has been subjected to the most barbaric, appalling and malicious campaign of slander . . . nothing can be gained by harping on about this matter, by pursuing something that just isn't there.'

Perhaps Ron Smith agreed. For he did not fly to Sydney to 'confront his daughter's killer' and present the 'damning new evidence' he had threatened. For whatever reason, he had second thoughts.

◻⧜◻

In August 1981, West Yorkshire coroner Philip Gill had refused to order an inquest into Helen Smith's death, deciding that the case did not fall within the jurisdiction of an English coroner's court. Helen's body had then been released for burial or cremation.

Ron Smith was not going to let his own grievance be buried though. He had pursued his quest so far it had become the centre of his life. Even when summonsed on one occasion to Leeds magistrates court for not paying his municipal rates, Ron Smith twice used the privilege of the court to accuse me of murdering Helen Smith. Of course, purely by chance, the gallery that day was full of reporters from the national media.

This inquest would end all that I hoped.

It was preposterous the way this man managed to unsettle even those in the highest positions; the British Foreign Office had taken the unprecedented step of publicly denying allegations made by Ron Smith and published in *Private Eye*.

It seemed nothing would deter Ron Smith. He had persisted in his long and hard drive for an inquest. Now, it seemed he had won. The Appeal Court of Great Britain ruled on 31 July 1982 that Ron Smith had the legal right to insist on an inquest.

My brother Nick phoned me, 'I believe it may be the first of its kind, in a case of someone dying abroad. A coroner normally holds an inquest for a death occurring in his jurisdiction. You've made history, Richard.'

Nick later discovered there had been a couple of precedents, inquests held on deaths that had occurred abroad, but those inquests had been held largely to help relatives obtain a death certificate. Such examples had been used by Ron Smith to justify an inquest into the death of his daughter.

Nevertheless, Helen Smith's inquest was indeed to make history and set a genuine precedent for other cases like it. Helen's case was taken to mean that an inquest had to be held for unnatural deaths occurring abroad. Indeed the British inquest years later into the deaths of Princess Diana and Dodi Fayed in Paris was a direct result of this.

'Quite frankly, the authorities must be looking for a way of shutting Ron Smith up,' Nick told me.

'Well, he's convinced of a cover-up, isn't he?'

'Ron Smith may be but the public certainly aren't. Oh, people are fascinated and intrigued by the big news all of this is making. But I've never come across a groundswell of opinion to the effect that the general public feel there was a cover-up. What is there to cover up, for goodness sake?'

Nick was appalled at the cost, and the wider implications for UK-Saudi relations. 'This whole thing is such a ridiculous expense, dragging witnesses here from all over the world. What a fuss he has caused, with all the stirring. Let's hope the inquest clears things up once and for all. Ron Smith wants it. The government wants it. The media want it. Have you any idea of the effect on our relationship with Saudi Arabia of this affair and the screening of "Death of a Princess"?'

◻↿◻

On 19 August 1982, I was sent a letter by the West Yorkshire Metropolitan Police asking me to 'give some indication' as to whether I would be prepared to attend an inquest into the death of Helen Smith at HM Coroner's Court in Leeds on 12 October.

Disregarding advice from friends and colleagues, I replied that I would be willing to attend but that I needed time in which to organise myself and hire a locum. I also requested that my expenses be paid – return air fares, travelling and living expenses in England, the cost of a locum, and legal expenses. Payment of some of these costs was agreed to.

I wrote to Saudi Arabia asking for the official police photographs of the two bodies. I pondered the silence surrounding the death of Johannes Otten. Why was there no inquest into his death? I had been told about Ron Smith tracking down Johannes' parents in Holland. They had already cremated their son's body.

The *Daily Mail* journalist Harry Longmuir wrote to alert me to an article published in the *Sunday Times* just prior to the inquest. In it, Ron Smith claimed he had enough prima facie evidence to implicate me, 'his daughter's lover', in her murder.

A surgical colleague in Britain wrote to me, saying he saw no possible use for an inquest 'other than serving as a platform for certain witnesses. It is just not possible to ascertain the cause of death on a body which has been eviscerated. The autopsy findings in Saudi Arabia are, by English law, hearsay only and the comments of subsequent eminent pathologists are valueless from the accounts I have seen of them.'

He continued his letter with the news that gossip still circulated about me. 'You have no doubt heard all the possible theories by now to account for the death of Helen Smith and the Dutch sea captain. The most favoured one is that the death of both of them occurred in a fracas in the flat during the party, started by an enraged and unsuccessful Saudi suitor.'

My brother wrote also, trying to persuade me that it would be a mistake to attend. 'The purpose of the inquest is solely to establish cause of death and, as you were asleep at the time, there is very little, if anything, your evidence can add in determining this point,' he wrote. Nick was not concerned about what might happen to me at the inquest but rather any problems I would face with publicity.

'That may fuel the fire of speculation. I do not see that your return to this country for the inquest will actually solve anything and the increased publicity would inevitably simply help to revive the story.'

His legal colleagues at the same time advised that my professional reputation might be affected. They recommended I seek assistance from the Medical Defence Union.

Another lawyer advised me against legal representation. He claimed it would convey the impression I needed legal protection. 'I question your wisdom in venturing into the lion's den,' he added.

回卍回

Other witnesses were contacted from all corners of the globe. Tim Hayter declined to attend. So did Penny. At around that time she married John Close and became a US citizen. From her home near Washington, she explained to Harry Longmuir why she would almost certainly refuse to attend the inquest. 'I have given the true version of all that happened on several occasions. I have not been believed by Helen's father and others,' she said. 'I can only repeat that same version at the inquest and I will still not be believed. And if I don't attend, it will be said I have something to hide, so I can't win either way.'

Newspapers reported that John Close's father, Ray, had been head of the CIA in the Middle East for several years. On his retirement Washington granted permission for Ray Close to continue working, but as employee of and chief adviser to the Saudis on all aspects of intelligence. All manner of wild rumours stemmed from that event. At one stage, I was accused by the media of being involved in espionage myself.

回卍回

The inquest was postponed for a few weeks because Ron Smith had applied for an order that it be heard by another coroner. He alleged Philip Gill was unsuitable because he had originally declined to hold an inquest. 'We've had a long and bitter correspondence over the past year,' Ron Smith told the newspapers, 'and I won't be happy with him in charge. I'll be suggesting that some other Yorkshire coroner take over the inquest.'

Ron Smith's High Court campaign over this was lost. The judge rejected Ron Smith's application and found that 'no reasonable man' could suspect Philip Gill would not be impartial.

Finally a date was set for the inquest; Thursday 18 November. By now, Ron Smith had begun to make public declarations of violence against me. I requested that action be taken to ensure my personal protection. Ron Smith continued with his tirades. He was adamant that the British Foreign Office and the Saudis were involved in a cover-up. He claimed the Thatcher government would fall if the facts of his daughter's death were revealed.

With a heavy heart I boarded my connecting flight for Sydney at Inverell. Margaret watched as I took off in the noisy Fokker Friendship. The red gravel of the bush runway rattled against its wings. Through a cloud of red dust my last sight was of Margaret, standing there, alone and forlorn.

The Final inquest

Early morning of 12 November in London was cold, grey and miserable. Looking down on the mass of little houses, the narrow streets and the traffic, and comparing the scene to the wide open spaces and sunshine of Inverell, I thought, 'Thank God I live a long way away from this'.

The leaden sky matched my mood. With a growing sense of apprehension I left the aircraft. My reception this time was quite different to that when I returned from Jeddah two years earlier.

'Please wait until all other passengers have disembarked,' the stewardess said. 'You are being met in the customs enclosure.'

I was relieved to be greeted by my brother Nick. 'I was hoping to get you out a back way,' he told me, 'but unfortunately I can't. We're going to have to leave by the front. There are heaps of journalists. We'll just have to make a run for it.'

We did, stepping into a blaze of television lights, camera flashes and microphones being thrust into my face. This was the beginning of a six weeks long firestorm of publicity.

The phalanx of journalists, at least a hundred this time, followed us, shouting out their questions.

'Why have you decided to attend the inquest?'

'What's it like to be back in Britain?'

'Can you tell us what happened at the party?'

They jostled, pushed and shoved as we tried to make our way through. They were anxious for answers, frantic for a story. In his keenness to photograph me, one fellow ran backwards, tripped over a cable and fell into a group of other press people.

We walked through the crowd, declining to comment, and ran

towards Nick's car which was parked nearby. The press throng chased us along the road but fortunately Nick managed to lose them in the traffic. He drove swiftly along the M4 motorway, weaving in and out of the rush hour vehicles.

'Nick, I had no idea there would be so much interest.'

'You can't say I didn't warn you. I'm getting calls from journalists at two or three o'clock in the morning. They give me a snippet of news they hope I haven't heard and try to get a reaction to it. They've behaved appallingly. I've had to learn to tell them to "push off",' he laughed.

I could not understand their continued interest. 'I'm amazed that the media find it so absorbing. The party was more than three years ago. Why are people still curious?'

It seemed that any whiff of a scandal or mystery and the press were hooked. I had Ron Smith to thank for that, and the pettiness of the media, who followed up his stupid tales. It was ludicrous. If people only knew how ordinary the circumstances of the party had really been. Scandal and mystery indeed.

'Where are the press cars, now?' I asked Nick, who was still driving fast along the M4.

'Don't worry, we've lost them for the time being,' he reassured me. 'You can relax, for a little while at least. We have an appointment with Sir David Napley later on today.'

◻️🔁◻️

We met Sir David at his chambers in Blackfriars in the City of London. I was immediately impressed. An elderly man, with thickset, prominent features and dark expressive eyes, he inspired immediate confidence. Sir David Napley was friendly and affable and regarded as one of the top solicitors in the country. He was a past president of the British Law Society. Nick had told me of his high profile, especially in the area of criminal matters. Well respected by his peers, he was known to the public mainly for having represented

Jeremy Thorpe, the former leader of the Liberal Party, at Thorpe's trial for attempted murder. (Sir David practised as a criminal solicitor, a branch of the law more common in the UK than in Australia.)

'Everyone else is being legally represented at this inquest and I fully agree with your brother, Nick, that you must also be,' he told me. 'Nick tells me you have shown the most remarkable fortitude, Richard. He says a weaker character could have easily been thrown off balance by the sort of experience you have been through. Would others have survived internment in a Saudi gaol as well as you did? Nick tells me you have always been a fighter, and that you are a very positive person. You will need that, Richard, to carry you through all this.'

'Well, let it now get me through the inquest,' I replied.

◧ ▣ ◨

After lunch at an excellent restaurant, we sat in Sir David's chambers. With clouds of smoke billowing from his meerschaum pipe, he turned to me and said, 'Richard, there is one thing you must understand.'

He was a grave man, and did not smile much.

'Some people say that I am the most expensive solicitor in London,' he continued, 'and I probably am, but I reckon to give first class service to all my clients.'

He paused. 'At the end of the day, you may have to pay my legal bill. Although the coroner has agreed to meet all your expenses, including your legal costs, there is no guarantee of this. You may end up having to pay my bill.

'Now is the time to decide whether you would like someone else to represent you. I'll be pleased to do so but you must understand that it is going to be expensive. If you have any doubts at all, now is the time to voice them and to find yourself a cheaper lawyer.'

My heart skipped a beat. I had not yet, more than two years after the event, been able to pay Dr al Sawaaf in Saudi Arabia for his work. But this was no time to falter, no time to quibble and be represented by less than the best.

'What sort of figure are you talking about?'

'At least twenty-five thousand pounds.'

I gulped. 'If I have to, I will pay your bill,' I promised Sir David. 'I will take that chance. I would like you to represent me.'

He gave me a small smile and shook my hand.

My legal costs alone were to come to over 32 000 pounds. My total costs were well over 50 000 pounds. The inquest must have cost at least half a million pounds; all on the British taxpayer.

Nick left then, and I then spent several hours with Sir David Napley and his assistant, lawyer Christopher Murray, a young, bright-eyed fellow who went through the details of the party meticulously, questioning me over and over again. By then exhaustion from the long flight was beginning to set in.

回리回

As I caught the train for the journey to my brother's Wincanton home at the end of the day, my stomach was churning and my head spinning with fatigue. I found the rush hour crowds quite daunting. Standing on the platform, despite wearing a thick coat and warm gloves, I shuddered with the horror of having to relive that dreadful time in Jeddah. Being woken early in the morning. The heart-stopping moment of seeing the two bodies, one of them gruesomely impaled on the fence.

Nick greeted me with the words, 'You look absolutely shattered,' as I walked through the door.

'And I feel it too,' I replied, gratefully sinking into a comfortable armchair.

'It was a good day, Richard, well worth your efforts. Sir David Napley wanted to be certain you were not withholding any information about the night and your interview certainly assured him of that. He feels comfortable, as I do, that this is all just nonsense, dreamt up by Ron Smith.'

During the days before the inquest, I visited my mother at Sheepscombe in the Cotswolds.

◧◪◨

The following few days were equally intense. Christopher Murray continued with my recollection of the events, all the time making copious notes. He presented me with stacks of press cuttings about the case and we diligently went through them together.

'Talk about one-sided publicity,' I commented.

'Yes, rather than a straightforward accident, the press has been whipped up to believe the party was some sort of sex orgy that had gone wrong and that the Foreign Office is trying to cover it up,' Christopher agreed.

'What is it that causes people to believe things are not really as simple and straightforward as they might be? Why is there a desire to believe things are much more wicked?' I asked.

'Human nature. And newspaper sales,' quipped Christopher Murray. 'This is a press-generated story, with a recipe of sex, violence and an exotic country. It has all the ingredients for a first rate scandal.'

After I had told Christopher all I knew, he started to prepare me for the inquest.

'The media think you will be accused directly by Ron Smith.'

'That's outrageous.'

'Maybe, but you must be prepared for it.'

I left his office feeling a mixture of shock, anxiety and anger. But it was too late for me to be having second thoughts now. I knew in my heart I had nothing to fear. Because I had not done anything wrong.

Sir David Napley offered me some final important words of advice. 'You are not here in the role of the defendant, Richard.

Remember that. An inquest is held where there is any indication of an unnatural death. But an inquest is not a court of law and you are not accused of anything. I am not here to defend you in that sense but to look after your interests.

'The sole purpose of an inquest is to ascertain a cause of death. An inquest never attempts to apportion blame. Anything relating to blame or to responsibility will be dealt with in another court. The inquest is purely to establish the cause of death,' he repeated.

I was to have cause to reflect on those words time and again.

Pressure was building. I was especially concerned at the proliferation and the vindictiveness of articles in *Private Eye*. They were attacking me as well as several others, from British Embassy officials to the coroner, Philip Gill. Stories about Helen's death often led the magazine. By now I was used to the slur of 'Death Party Doctor'. I was therefore not surprised to see myself featured on the cover of issue 546, dated 19 November. 'Dr Arnot flies in' was the caption under a photograph of me arriving at Heathrow. The balloon from my mouth read, 'When it's all over I'm going to throw a party'.

◫◪◫

I drove to Yorkshire, with Sir David Napley at the wheel of his gold Rolls Royce, smoking his pipe. We were accompanied by his wife Leah, a quietly spoken, intelligent and elegant woman, and Christopher Murray.

We drove through Leeds, where the inquest was to be held, and on to Harrogate, some twenty minutes on, where we booked into the Old Swan Hotel, a grand establishment of the Victorian era.

'With all the media interest, the further we stay out of Leeds, the better,' explained Sir David. 'It is important to have some privacy at a time like this.'

He was right.

It was clear that Sir David liked to do things in style. He enjoyed good food and good wine and made sure that we frequented the best restaurants the area had to offer. While I had initially thought that the proceedings would take a couple of days, Sir David had blocked off a month in his appointment book.

Again he was right. Far nearer the mark than I. We spent the evening prior to the start of the inquest in Sir David's room, chatting comfortably in a relaxed atmosphere. There was no tension. Not then.

I slept well and awoke feeling fresh and at ease on the morning of Thursday 18 November. The hotel boasted a delicious full breakfast. I ate heartily – bacon and eggs and kippers.

It was hard to believe that there had ever been such a concentration of lawyers and witnesses in the history of British inquests.

Ron Smith was represented by a keen young Geoffrey Robertson in the early years of his prestigious career. Geoffrey Robertson was already well known for having advised the Australian defendants in the Oz trial. Other members of Helen's family also had a barrister representing their interests, Stephen Sedley. He was acting for Helen Smith's mother, Jeryl Sheehy, who did not attend the inquest.

Now remarried and living in America, she appointed her son David as her representative. The two barristers, Christopher Murray explained to me, were there either because family interests were not mutual or because they wanted to have the opportunity of asking twice the number of questions.

'Is that unusual?' I asked.

'The whole case is unusual, Richard,' he said. 'In ninety-nine per cent of inquests, there would probably be no legal representation at all. It would all be very straightforward with no issue over the cause of death.'

A bevy of Treasury lawyers attended on behalf of the British Government, and sat together in their dark suits, not participating in any way. I seem to recall that several of the Germans also had legal representation.

All the survivors of the fateful party had been asked to attend and every one did, with the notable exception of Tim Hayter and Penny. Various representatives of the British Embassy in Jeddah were present, including the consul, Francis Geere, and the military attaché, Murray de Klee.

On the first morning, we pulled up slowly in front of Leeds Town Hall. Sir David parked by the main steps. We were immediately mobbed by the press. 'Don't react to them,' Sir David advised, 'just smile and walk straight ahead.' I was surprised at the small army of journalists, photographers and television crews lining the steps. Now I realised why this venue had been chosen in preference to the smaller coroner's court. Reporters and camera crews rushed to the car, hardly giving us a chance to get out, shoving microphones and cameras at us and showering us with questions.

'No comment,' responded Sir David politely. We walked, three abreast, past the large crowd attracted by the activity and TV cameras.

We walked up the stairs of the town hall, across its splendid entrance lobby and into a small anteroom, where we hung our coats, before proceeding into the Council Chamber set aside for the inquest.

The coroner sat up fairly high, above several rows of benches. Journalists were perched in the gallery above him. It was standing room only; the hall was packed, with a great line of people queuing for public seats. There was a huge buzz, a colossal amount of interest.

I chose a seat towards the back. Sir David and Christopher Murray sat in front of me.

Ron Smith walked past, his two sons, David and Graham, by his side. He had lost weight and looked thin and gaunt. His hair was longer and greyer. He was busy chatting to everyone in sight.

A wave of loathing flashed through my body, a feeling of intense hostility. This was the man who had caused me and my family so much distress, so much pain. He appeared not to see me. The small group sat down several rows in front of me and to the left.

I suppose it would have been no more than a matter of five or ten minutes before the coroner, Philip Gill, entered and the proceedings commenced. In a soft but firm voice, he announced the start of the inquest into the death of Helen Smith and said he would be calling witnesses. He would begin with medical evidence about the state of her body, evidence to be provided by the three pathologists who had carried out the post mortems.

That was my first shock. 'Why don't they call the other witnesses first and ask what happened at the party?' I whispered to Sir David Napley and Christopher Murray. 'Isn't this putting the cart before the horse?'

The first witness called was pathologist Dr Michael Green from Leeds University's Department of Forensic Medicine. He had carried out the third post mortem on Helen Smith, on 27 June 1980, over a year after she had died. At that time Dr Green stated he had been unable to establish the cause of death with certainty as the internal organs had been removed in Saudi Arabia after the second post mortem.

Dr Green now began his evidence, explaining how Helen Smith's body showed indications of mould and insect activity and that the body was extensively decomposed. At this, several members of the public blanched.

Producing notes of his post mortem findings, he said he had noted injuries around Helen Smith's genital region but had not included them in his report on the instruction of the coroner at the time. Coroner Miles Coverdale deemed these injuries to have no direct bearing on the cause of death and felt they would cause Helen's family unnecessary distress. There were several gasps of surprise at this revelation.

Dr Green went on to describe bruises on the inside of the thigh. Yes, they could be caused by one leg slapping against another during a fall, he said on questioning, but his thought was that the bruising was more consistent with forced sexual intercourse.

Dr Green concluded that the principal injuries – fractures of the right pelvis, shoulder and eighth rib and extensive bruising – were consistent with a fall from a moderate height but that others were indicative of some form of rough handling or assault prior to death. (How anyone could draw such conclusions from a long dead, decomposed body was beyond me.)

The next post mortem had taken place on 16 December 1980. The pathologists were Dr Green, Professor Joergen Dalgaard (on behalf of Ron Smith), and Professor Alan Usher, for coroner Miles Coverdale. Dr Green summarised the findings of this post mortem: that the head and face injuries had occurred during life, most likely from slaps or blows, that there were injuries consistent with forced sexual intercourse and that there was no scar present from an appendicectomy (which had taken place a few weeks before Helen died).

All of this conflicted with my recollection of what Helen Smith had looked like soon after death. All I had seen was the slight dent on the right side of her forehead. There was no visible bruising. There were no cuts. No abrasions. No facial or head wounds. I remembered questioning the lack of visible injuries at the time.

Geoffrey Robertson and Stephen Sedley pressed Dr Green. He admitted he had incorrectly noted a sub-capital fracture of the right humerus. A lesion of the head, which he had previously attributed to hair dye, could instead have been a wound. He agreed with Geoffrey Robertson's suggestion that such a wound could have been caused by violence. He agreed with Stephen Sedley's suggestion that Helen's body, in a state of half undress, was a typical picture of a rape victim.

What was I hearing? This could not be. As Dr Green was being questioned about the lack of an appendicectomy scar, I started to doubt my own memory. All the more so when Sir David turned back in his seat to face me with an amazed look and and said, 'You told us you took her appendix out yourself.'

'I did,' I assured him. In my mind's eye, I could visualise the operation. I could see Helen in bed recovering. I could see her sitting on our couch talking to my mother-in-law about it, showing her the scar. I could clearly see the whole sequence of events.

However, there were two difficulties; the absence of any hospital records, and the absence of the internal organs.

Sir David Napley rose. His questioning was polite but incisive, firm yet penetrating. He described the damaged state of Helen Smith's internal organs, as noted by the Saudi Arabian pathologist at the autopsy in Jeddah. Dr Green agreed that such injuries were consistent with a fall from seventy feet (twenty-one metres).

Then Sir David asked a vital question; could the marks on Helen's body be post mortem artefacts, caused by drying out or handling of the body? Dr Green disagreed with this. He thought the marks had been sustained during life. He also disagreed with Sir David's suggestion that Helen Smith had fallen on top of Johannes Otten, thus lessening her injuries. No, Dr Green believed the bodies had separated on falling.

That was one of the worst days of my life. I was extremely uneasy about the pathology evidence. 'It doesn't agree with what I saw,' I told Sir David and Christopher Murray. 'It doesn't add up. They are coming to the wrong conclusions.'

'That's up to the coroner to decide,' said Sir David.

That evening we walked out of Leeds Town Hall, into the dark, cold air and the heat from television lights and the barrage of journalists' questions.

'How do you think it's going?'

'How do you feel?'

Sir David had difficulty backing his large car out of the tight parking space; he was further impeded by the reporters clustering around. 'Get out of the way,' he muttered.

There were even more members of the public crowded around, and more policemen to keep them in order. It was a relief to get away from it all.

Back in the hotel, we watched the evening news; again I was surprised at how much prominence was being given to the case and the inquest. I slept badly that night, tossing and turning, and awoke feeling more apprehensive than ever.

The morning newspapers had a field day. Dr Green's post mortem findings had been reported at the time they were made. However, the Helen Smith case had since gained momentum and ever-increasing attention. In addition, this medical professional now admitted to having suppressed some of his findings. Such a disclosure proved there had indeed been a cover-up of some sort.

◨◧◩

Next day saw the Saudi pathologist Dr Ali Mohammed Kheir give his evidence. Dr Kheir had carried out the second post mortem on Helen's body, in Jeddah on 2 June 1979. A short, stocky fellow, he was not fluent in English and spoke through an interpreter.

Post mortems were uncommon in Saudi Arabia. The first post mortem on Helen had been simply an external examination of the body. Then after Ron Smith arrived in Jeddah, and insisted, a second, full, post mortem had been carried out. It was then that the internal organs had been removed, and the body cavities filled with sawdust, mothballs and charcoal.

I have no idea why the internal organs were removed in Saudi. In England and Australia, internal organs would have been examined, portions sectioned and examined microscopically, but they would then have been replaced in the body.

I remember there being a general feeling of embarrassment that Dr Kheir's post mortem had been so perfunctory, that he had done so little. He gave the impression his main interest was to establish whether or not Helen had been pregnant. He commented that her nipples were of a pale pink colour, it being believed that the nipples of pregnant women darkened.

'For goodness sake, if Helen Smith died having intercourse, as all the evidence suggests, why is he worrying about any signs of pregnancy?' I asked Sir David.

There was positive evidence of semen being present in her vagina and there was alcohol in her blood.

Dr Kheir said he was satisfied that the bodies had fallen from the balcony and doubted that Helen Smith had been sexually assaulted. Then came a bombshell, under intense questioning by Geoffrey Robertson.

From the final position of the bodies, Dr Kheir concluded that Johannes Otten had fallen at speed, possibly the result of running. Maybe after having been pushed?

Naturally the media seized on this.

I remember there was some consternation when Dr Kheir admitted he had carried out a post mortem on Johannes Otten. Until then, no one was aware of that. But this information did not come to much, because Dr Kheir did not have the report with him.

On being questioned by Sir David, he repeated that Helen Smith's injuries were consistent with a fall. He had seen nothing to indicate a conclusion other than death caused by accidental injury.

That afternoon, it was the turn of the Danish pathologist Dr Joergen Dalgaard to present his evidence. Professor of Forensic Medicine at the University of Aarhus, Dr Dalgaard had been approached by Ron Smith to take on the role of independent pathologist. Dr Dalgaard's were the most sensational words yet.

Fluent and confident in English, he spoke loudly in an accented voice. A fairly well-built man, his white hair and stern face gave him a dignified air, increased by his dramatic presentation. He spoke from his copious notes and gesticulated freely.

As far as I knew, forensic evidence was something finite and concrete, based on observed facts, not tailored to fit theories. I was surprised to find that Professor Dalgaard appeared to be trying to fit in his findings, and explain them in terms of Ron Smith's theories. Dr Dalgaard made a great issue of a couple of marks he had noticed on the front of Helen Smith's neck. He said these were consistent with thumb and fingerprint marks, as if somebody had been trying to strangle her.

'We've heard Dr Green tell us how extensively decomposed the body was,' I whispered to Sir David Napley. 'How can Dr Dalgaard draw those inferences? His evidence does not resemble the forensic deduction I have known before.'

How I regretted, too, not having insisted on a witness being present at the post mortems on my own behalf. The other evidence, as it progressed, continued to fill me with a sense of quiet rage.

Professor Dalgaard maintained a large injury on the left side of the head, and the resulting cerebral haemorrhage, had been caused by a blow to the head, most likely from an open hand. He further stated that the small amount of injury sustained by Helen Smith was not consistent with a fall from twenty metres, but rather from a far more moderate height, perhaps three metres, from the balcony of a first floor flat.

There was a deathly hush in the hall while Dalgaard spoke. Immediately afterwards, a general buzz of conversation began. There was great activity in the press gallery, journalists constantly coming and going, obviously wanting to be the first to break the sensational news.

Sir David got straight to the crux of the matter. He asked Dr Dalgaard why he thought Helen Smith may have fallen from a first floor flat. Dalgaard told Sir David that Ron Smith had told him Helen may have been there that night. I wondered to myself, can no one else detect how he is tailoring his findings to Ron Smith's stories?

Dr Dalgaard said the bruises and marks on Helen's body were due to violence before death. I sat in the body of the Council Chamber, seething. The bruises and marks were not present when I saw Helen's body an hour or two after she died. Dr Dalgaard was talking about minute observations made on a decomposed and eviscerated corpse eighteen months after death. How could anyone draw such precise conclusions?

Smith's lawyers amplified these erroneous conclusions in their questioning. They brought out again the lack of an appendicectomy scar.

That afternoon, too, we discovered why Dr Dalgaard was going on about a first floor balcony. It seemed that was where Dr Sarchal, an Iranian, lived. According to her father, Helen was having an affair with him. A *Sunday Times* article had quoted Ron Smith as saying that he thought Helen died in Dr Sarchal's flat. Conveniently for the conspiracy theorists, Sarchal had left Jeddah the day after Helen's death. (Later in the inquest, in sworn evidence, it transpired that Sarchal had gone on pre-arranged recreational leave that day.)

I constantly discussed with my legal representatives my misgivings about the evidence being presented. 'It is very important that you realise why you are here,' Christopher Murray reminded me. 'Don't go on the defensive.'

Despite the unpleasant events each day, Sir David, his wife Leah and Christopher made sure the evenings were not sombre. These men were used to dealing with high-profile cases, where emotions ran high. That was the nature of their work. They walked away from it at the end of the day and, instead of dwelling on what had happened, they thought out and planned for the next day.

Professor Alan Usher from Sheffield was the fourth pathologist to give evidence. He said it was pure speculation that Helen had been raped or violently attacked before her death. In his opinion, enthusiastic and vigorous sexual intercourse could have caused the injuries in her genital area and her total injuries could only have been sustained in a fall of twenty metres, not less. On questioning by Geoffrey Robertson, he said he was surprised that Helen Smith's sternum or breastbone had been fractured and agreed this could have occurred in an attempt made to resuscitate her.

Now the pathologists claim that the sternum is one of the hardest bones to break, that it requires tremendous force! I thought to myself, sternums often fracture. I had seen it in my own patients. But my mute protestations were futile. The following day, the newspapers spoke of 'desperate efforts possibly having been made on dying nurse'.

By then my anger was turning to despondency. A few days into the inquest, I rang Margaret who was still in Australia, and asked, 'Please come over.'

◻⊡◻

Sir David was not one to talk in the morning. He had four or five daily newspapers delivered and he read them over breakfast. One morning, he peered over the paper he was holding and said to me, 'You know, Richard, I think you're attending the wrong inquest. I've just been reading about an inquest in Leeds and it's certainly not the one that I recollect happening yesterday.'

The journalist had written his piece out of context. He had sensationalised it. He had seized on some little insignificant point and made much of it.

Sir David was being ironical. But he was angry that the media were reporting inaccurately, and treating the issues so superficially.

◻⊡◻

Turning up in style as we did every day, caused a stir. The media played up the contrasts. They cast us as the British establishment in a case against the working class man, the battler. Sir David was pictured in his dapper winter coat and brown bowler hat emerging from his luxurious vehicle, dubbed 'The Golden Roller' by the press, while Ron Smith walked along wearing a scruffy old raincoat, tied around the waist with a piece of string.

As the days went by, I found Ron Smith to be an increasingly strange man. We never spoke to each other during the three weeks of the inquest. But one lunchtime as we were walking out of the hall, Ron Smith caught my eye and gave me a huge wink. I was astonished; I thought, 'You cynical bastard. You're the man who has caused all this problem. What are you doing, winking at me?'

It was a friendly wink, a totally out of place gesture given the circumstances. Other than that wink, he never acknowledged me in any way.

◻⊡◻

Dr Alan Kirwin was called and told the inquest of how he had supplied whisky on the day of the party and briefly attended the evening's activities. All the Germans gave evidence, except for Dieter Chapuis who was working in Iraq and sent a written statement which was read out. They spoke of the pleasant friendly party that had no hint of any fight or violence.

As Manfred Schlaefer was being questioned by one of the other barristers, Ron Smith suddenly leapt to his feet. 'I accuse Richard Arnot and Jacques Texier of murdering my daughter.'

Sir David was on his feet immediately, 'That is an outrageous accusation and I demand it be withdrawn.'

Journalists rushed to the phones. Ron Smith's outburst was the news of the day. The coroner, Philip Gill, later rebuked him for contempt, and demanded he produce evidence to show Jacques Texier had been involved in his daughter's murder. I, meantime, could speak for myself when my turn came.

Jacques Texier was not able to respond directly to the attack. He was still in Jeddah, unable to be released from his work contract. He had provided a statement to be read out in his absence.

Unable to produce any such evidence from his client, Geoffrey Robertson was subdued. But Ron Smith's words were inadvertently to bring about Jacques Texier's attendance.

On reading the accusation against her son, Jacques' mother suffered a heart attack. Jacques rushed to her side in France and then came on to Leeds. Jacques' evidence was to prove to be most pertinent. He had, after all, remained in the flat after all the Germans had gone.

Before Jacques made his appearance, however, Murray de Klee and several Foreign Office officials, including Gordon Kirby, gave their evidence. Francis Geere entered the witness stand as did the Bakhsh Hospital employees, including matron Agnes Johnstone, anaesthetist Dr Keith, and his wife, Kathleen. Statements from Drs Bakhsh, Rakhman and Sukhtian were read out.

Kathleen Keith, who had lived on the floor below ours, spoke of the loud noise she had heard on the night of 19-20 May while attending to her sick toddler.

Some witnesses spoke of Helen's appendicectomy. Now I understood the fascination with this operation I had carried out and the attempts to discredit me. The speculation was that this had been merely cover for an abortion.

Was I being depicted as a hard impassive man? Had I been, was I too controlled in my emotions? Early on in a doctor's career he learns how to control many emotions and feelings. When the inquest heard grisly details – such as how it had taken one or two hours to saw through the railings and remove Johannes Otten's impaled body – as the public and the jury cringed and the media lapped up the particulars, I sat impassively, staring ahead.

When a patient died, I always felt a personal sense of loss. Whether that patient had been young or old, terminally ill or not, there was always the sense of loss, even if death was inevitable. In my profession, I had to learn to cope with sickness and with death. It was all around me. You felt sad but you had to learn to take it in your stride, to cope, to get on with the next patient. To a certain extent, one had to develop a kind of impersonal, a sort of dispassionate look. Even though there was a degree of emotion involved, one had to control that, keep it in check, stand back a bit and say the things that needed to be said, without becoming too involved oneself.

回己回

By now Margaret had arrived. Having her by my side made all the difference. Support also came unexpectedly. From the crowd, which never dwindled during the days of the inquest, came shouts of encouragement. One person in particular, a short, slight woman, perhaps in her fifties, often caught my eye and smiled at me. Towards the end of the inquest, she grasped my hand as I walked by and thrust a note into it. Handwritten, on blue lined notepaper, it read: 'Dear Dr Arnot, I thought you'd like to know that I admired you through all this. Just keep your chin up.' And she had signed her name.

◰◱◰

Ron Smith took the stand at long last. How I had been waiting for this. He would finally back up all his allegations, or so I thought. Smith was unhappy at having to give his evidence before I gave mine, and started by asking Philip Gill for permission to make a statement. Permission declined, he took no notice and, with the coroner interrupting, declared he would not talk about what had occurred between the hours of 2 a.m. and 5 a.m. on 20 May 1979 until I had presented my evidence.

In his one and a half hours in the witness box, Ron Smith described how the 'perfect' state of his daughter's body convinced him she had not fallen from a height of twenty metres. 'She looked as though she had just laid down – she looked as though she had fallen asleep.'

Although he claimed to have evidence that Helen had fallen from another balcony, he refused to elaborate. Instead he said, 'There is evidence to indicate not only Helen but Richard Arnot was in another flat and Jacques Texier and one or two others. I will go into that when Richard Arnot has been in the box.'

Everyone looked with expectation at Sir David.

'No questions,' he snapped and a surprised Ron Smith stepped down from the witness box.

The next day, Thursday 2 December, it was my turn to appear. I have to admit I felt slightly let down by Sir David Napley. When I gave my evidence, I expected him to lead me, as it were, to ask certain questions that would develop certain points. It could have been an opportunity to comment on some of the conclusions drawn by the pathologists, to bring out the question of whether or not Helen had undergone an appendicectomy. My evidence could have gone some way towards discrediting the forensic evidence.

But Sir David did not do that. He didn't think it was necessary. 'You didn't need any support at all, Richard,' he told me, 'your evidence was absolutely immaculate.'

I had been warned by Sir David Napley. I had forgotten his advice. I had inadvertently slipped into the role of defendant in my expectations of him.

While Ron Smith's evidence had been somewhat of an anticlimax, mine included a new disclosure – that Penny and Tim Hayter had had sex that night. This fact had not been made public before and caused much interest, especially as Penny and I had not mentioned it in the *Daily Mail* articles.

I described the party – 'pleasant and convivial', the discovery of the bodies – 'grotesque and nauseating', and how Tim had confessed to me. Seizing on my wife's adulterous behaviour, Geoffrey Robertson suggested this had not happened and was merely an alibi for murder.

I strenuously rejected this and explained how she had retracted her admission to the Saudi authorities in order to avoid capital punishment.

And why had she continued to deny her adulterous behaviour after returning to Britain?

'She was acutely ashamed and embarrassed.'

Asked about my response to her behaviour, I admitted I felt very let down.

On further questioning by Geoffrey Robertson, I acknowledged payment for the *Daily Mail* articles. 'When I came back to Britain, I had debts amounting to £10 000. I had been unable to work for eighteen months. We were pursued by journalists from all over the country, sums being mentioned to us in excess of £50 000. We spoke to the *Daily Mail* for a figure which was nothing like that amount.'

I told of the balcony that we had regarded as highly dangerous, explaining how its tiled floor would have been extremely slippery to anyone in bare feet and perspiring in any way.

When it came to my description of the bodies, Geoffrey Robertson referred to Johannes Otten's erection, asking, 'Doctor, do you think sexual activity is possible after death?'

It seemed a particularly silly question at the time.

'As far as I am aware, active participation in sexual activity ceases at the moment of death,' I answered.

There were a few titters and some nervous laughter. Geoffrey Robertson blushed.

I was in the witness box for one and a half days. The papers wrote of my 'loud clear voice that never faltered'.

Although Penny and Tim Hayter had chosen not to attend the inquest, their evidence did not go unheard. Penny's statement made to the West Yorkshire Metropolitan Police on 27 August 1980 was read out, and a television interview with Tim Hayter shown to the jury.

Then it was the turn of the final witness. When Jacques Texier took the stand, he described the party, seeing Helen Smith and Johannes Otten step out on to the balcony and his embarrassment at waking up in the night, to the sound of Penny and Tim's love-making. He laughed off suggestions that he was a mercenary soldier, and waved a newspaper in Ron Smith's direction. 'They say we are from an intelligence service and we killed a spy – Mr Otten – and we killed Miss Smith because she was a witness.'

Ron Smith made no further attempt to present evidence.

Philip Gill's summing up took more than a day. The end was in sight. Then would come the decision of the jury as to the cause of Helen Smith's death.

I was tired. I was irritable. I was looking forward to the conclusion of the inquest.

The coroner had taken an active part in the proceedings, constantly asking questions, clarifying points and making notes. Now he presented a most detailed summing up that even included his own theory of events.

He suggested to the jury that the three European pathologists had been misled by marks on Helen Smith's body, marks not seen by the Jeddah pathologist, Dr Ali Mohammed Kheir. Perhaps they were marks made after death, by the handling of the body in the mortuary, in the holding and supporting of the head.

Philip Gill speculated that Johannes Otten's trousers had been taken by a passer-by as was his wallet containing a deal of money.

He postulated that Helen Smith and Johannes Otten had been making love on the balcony and, on hearing the sounds of his friends leaving below, Johannes had rushed over with Helen to ask them to wait, tripped over the sun lounger and the two of them had fallen to their deaths.

The jury had to make one of three possible decisions – unlawful killing, accidental death or, if there was insufficient evidence to reach a clear conclusion, an open verdict.

The jury retired to consider their verdict late in the morning of Thursday 9 December. They returned, to great anticipation, late that afternoon. But they only wanted to ask a question.

'If a fall had happened as a result of sexual activity of an aggressive nature, would that be considered unlawful killing or accidental death?' asked the female jury foreman.

'Unlawful killing' if the fall had occurred as the result of rape or assault and 'accidental death' if it was consensual sexual activity on the part of the woman, answered the coroner.

A couple of hours later the foreperson returned, saying the jury was unable to reach a unanimous decision. Philip Gill explained he could accept a majority decision if there were no more than two dissents. This was not the case and the jury left for further deliberation. My anxiety level was building.

Finally, an hour later, after almost seven hours of deliberation, the jury gave its decision.

'Open verdict.'

I felt let down. There had been this colossal effort, this enormous amount of energy expended, time and money spent and all for an open verdict.

'It's exactly as I had expected. It was a fair verdict,' said Sir David.

'I'm disappointed,' I told him, 'I had hoped we would come to a conclusion. A verdict of accidental death.'

'The evidence was so vague and incomplete, that was not possible,' Christopher Murray explained. 'You should be relieved that there was no direct evidence to show Helen Smith had been unlawfully killed, as Ron Smith claims.'

I walked out of Leeds Town Hall, disappointed that suspicion would remain about the death of Helen Smith. Nevertheless, I was pleased it was all over.

And it was all over. Even *Private Eye* dropped the issue stone dead, and turned their attention to something else.

回凸回

Back at his London office, we said goodbye to Sir David. He presented me with a copy of his memoirs. On the front page, he wrote, 'Richard, a reminder of the vindication of a kind, able and conscientious man.'

Epilogue

Margaret and I were married, on 6 September 1982 at Casino, Margaret's home town. The press again had a field day. One journalist travelled from England for the event. He woke me up early one morning, demanding an exclusive interview. He turned up at the ceremony and took photographs which were plastered over the British papers.

I have a new life now with my new family; my wife Margaret and our three children. In some ways, it is the life I was denied before; watching my children grow up and be educated, and develop into mature and responsible members of society.

My relationship with the children of my first marriage, William and Lucy, has been strained and interrupted. I regret that. I would like them to read my story – the tale of one man's personal fall and rebirth. Despite having been through such an awful experience, it is possible to recover and make a good life, indeed a much better life for oneself.

Getting everything into focus, letting it ferment and fall into place has brought back many distressing and painful issues with which I had to deal. Now that time has passed and eased my pain, I have got things into better perspective. I want this book to be the record of events that I and others believe were totally distorted by Ron Smith and the British media.

I am aiming for an honest book, one that may inspire others in difficult situations. And I am not looking to criticise Saudi Arabia, but rather to highlight the paradoxes that exist there.

Each year, around the anniversary of Helen's death, there is usually a small flurry of interest. I may be contacted by media and asked to comment. Every year or two I see an article featuring Ron Smith and his latest theory. These are all pinpricks to me now, small reminders of a curiosity that still continues. I don't think media interest will go away completely until Ron Smith dies.

He is the person whom I feel most sorry for in all of this. If one is to believe what one reads in the paper, his life is totally wrecked. The death of Helen has dogged his life as he searches for something that doesn't exist, unwilling to accept that her demise was a tragic accident. He is an old man now, an old and bitter man who has lost everything – his family, his life, his money.

To me, one of the most cruel aspects is that Helen Smith is still unburied, at the time of writing, mid-1998. Nineteen years after her death, her body still lies in the mortuary at Leeds General Infirmary – a symbol of her father's obsession, and the result of a promise made to Ron Smith by the Leeds Health Trust to cover storage costs. In great distress, Helen's mother has begged that her daughter's remains be laid to rest.

Until Ron Smith accepts the truth of the accident, he will not be able to say goodbye to his daughter. I have heard that he is still pushing to see 'justice done', pushing for the case to be re-opened, reminding British Prime Minister Tony Blair of a promise made to him in 1983 by Michael Foot, the then leader of the Labour Party, that a Labour government would 'look into every aspect of the case'.

As for myself, I have found tremendous support in Inverell. People stop me in the street and chat. I feel at home here. It is my home. I continue to enjoy the combination of a busy surgical practice with a country lifestyle and have been able to realise my dream of flying. During my time in gaol, I learnt a lot about myself. After it was all over, small things didn't seem to be that important any more. Situations which I would previously have found intimidating, now don't bother me in the slightest.

Coming to Australia, where there is much more egalitarianism, made the difference. Here I find it very pleasant being able to relate to people on first-name terms, even if they are somewhat older and more senior.

Coping with difficulties that might have intimidated or broken some people, I felt confidence in myself at having survived.

After having been in gaol, I noticed that I took far more pleasure just out of people's presence. I talk to people and listen to people from all walks of life and greatly enjoy their company.

The whole thing seems almost like a bad dream now. I remember Helen and I am truly sorry that she died. She was a girl who took all sorts of chances. She enjoyed fun, she certainly enjoyed a bit of drinking. She moved through life fairly fast, and I guess that night in Jeddah was just one move too many.

Standing on my verandah in Inverell today and looking out on to the green paddocks before me, the desert plains of Jeddah seem far away. Were Helen to walk up to me now, what would I say to her?

Only this, 'Oh Helen, it's good to see you again.'

May her spirit rest in peace.